That Hideous Strength: How the West was Lost

What people are saying about this book...

Within a framework established by reference to C.S. Lewis' *That Hideous Strength* and the Genesis Tower of Babel, Tinker challenges the church and its leaders to look full in the face at the cultural forces that are carrying us all on into a brave new world. The dreams of cultural Marxism are to a considerable extent becoming realities in one realm after another, notably in the sexual realm and in the emergence of new totalitarian tendencies seeking to control what we say and think. We freshly face a situation in which Christians will need to stand up and be counted. Trust in God needs to lead to invested thinking and action. This is a timely book that deserves to be widely attended to.

Professor John Nolland, Trinity College Bristol

The last sixty years have witnessed the death in the West of the Judeo-Christian worldview and its replacement by an increasingly totalitarian secularism. Melvin Tinker deftly explains how this revolution happened, and exposes the tactics that enabled Cultural Marxism to triumph amongst our institutions and elites. We are deceiving ourselves if we think that this new ideology is simply about achieving equality.

Rather it seeks the abolition of the family as the basis for society. Having identified the challenge he helpfully shows how Christians should respond. Following in the footsteps of William Wilberforce we must proclaim the gospel of God and vigorously refute the ideas and values of the present day. He calls for bold and courageous evangelical leadership, which is often sadly lacking in the contemproary church. Although a challenging read, this book provides invaluable help in understanding our contemporary context. It will make you grieve, pray and deepen your confidence in the gospel of the Lord Jesus, which is alone able to free lost men and women from their bondage to sin and Satan.

John Stevens FIEC

It is rare to find forensic intelligence and spiritual acuity in one person and one place. In this excellent study, drawing on the analysis and discernment of CS Lewis, Melvin Tinker identifies one of the greatest dangers orthodox Christianity faces. If this book manages to wake the Church to the danger it faces it will have done a great service to the Kingdom of heaven today. It is a great strength of the book that interpreting and applying Lewis' analysis, it offers not only a warning, but also an antidote.

Bishop Gavin Ashenden

A very brave, fine book written with keen insight. It explains how an older worldview that once shaped the West and in which many Judeo-Christian ideas were embedded has been superseded by one in which those ideas have been uprooted. The brave new world which is dawning is one in which people liberate themselves, dominate the meaning of reality, and subject God— if he is still there—to their own ends. In this context, the church is in a decidedly countercultural position. It is here, though, that it really finds its voice. Here it is able to speak into our fragile and corrupting world and speak of the goodness, greatness and grace of God.

David F. Wells, Distinguished Research Professor,
Gordon-Conwell Theological Seminary

We live in interesting times, times of rapid change where all that is solid seems truly to be melting into air. And, rather than be appalled by this, many in the West greet it as something great and good, even as the magnificent end of history. Melvin Tinker disagrees, and is right to do so. In this brief but pungent critique of our current cultural pathologies, he exposes how stories—the wrong stories—have come to grip our imaginations, how cultural politics has redrawn the map of perceived reality, and how only the story of Jesus Christ and his church can truly satisfy humanity's deepest longings, intellectual and spiritual.

Carl R Trueman, Professor of Biblical and Religious
Studies, Grove City College, USA

In this short work, Melvin Tinker has shown what lies at the heart of our post-modern malaise. The grand project of attacking and deconstructing natural social forms, such as the family, then goes on to the constructivist where human identity and social identity becomes largely what we choose to make it. Tinker tells us that our elite have been enamoured of this project for several generations and have thus caused incalculable harm to vital social and national institutions. For the author, however, the true overarching narrative begins in eternity and has its fulfilment in Jesus Christ as the meaning and goal of history.

Bishop Michael Nazir-Ali

That Hideous Strength: How the West was Lost

The Cancer of Cultural Marxism in the Church
and the World, and the Gospel of Change

Melvin Tinker

EP BOOKS
1st Floor Venture House, 6 Silver Court, Watchmead, Welwyn
Garden City, UK, AL7 1TS

www.epbooks.org
admin@epbooks.org

EP Books are distributed in the USA by:
JPL Books, 3883 Linden Ave. S.E.,
Wyoming, MI 49548

www.jplbooks.com
orders@jplbooks.com

First edition published 2018

ISBN: 978-1-78397-240-1

British Library Cataloguing in Publication Data available

To Don and Joy Carson

With gratitude for modelling how to apply
the whole of Bible to the whole of life

Contents

Foreword

RECENTLY AN AVERSION TO USING THE LANGUAGE OF 'culture wars' has appeared in British Christian circles. It may be a justified reaction to a particular American discourse and partisan politicization of the gospel message, which in terms of our communication to the non-Christian world, *can* come across as somewhat simplistic and shrill. However, one problem with the reaction against 'culture war' language is that theologically it's at odds with a constant biblical theme from Genesis to Revelation which delineates a fundamental distinction between human beings, what theologians call 'the antithesis.' The second chapter of Colossians summarises this well when it talks about two, *and only two*, types of people: those have received Jesus Christ as Lord, rooted and built up in him, and those 'not according to Christ' who are captive through hollow and deceptive philosophy, which depend on human tradition and the elemental spiritual forces. The truth that all humans beings are made in God's image, and the truth that as Christians we are to love our enemies *does not* negate the reality of the God-given 'enmity' (Gen.

3:15) between those who worship Christ and those who worship idols.

Like it or not, Christians are engaged in a religious war, a war of competing worldviews—fundamentally different ways of interpreting the world which impact our lives now and with eternal consequences. As has been pointed out, like wearing a pair of glasses, we don't see these worldviews because we see *with* them. As Roy Clouser has pointed out in his 1991 book *The Myth of Religious Neutrality*:

> The enormous influence of religious beliefs remains, however, largely hidden from causal; its relation to the rest of life is like that of the great geological plates of earth's surface to the continents and oceans. The movement of these plates is not apparent to a causal inspection of any particular landscape can only be detected with great difficulty. Nevertheless, so vast are these plates, so stupendous their power, that their visible effects— mountain ranges, earthquakes, and volcanic eruptions—are but tiny surface blemishes compared with the force of the mighty plates themselves.

With the help of C.S. Lewis, this book is a creative exercise of looking at the world through the Word and focusing on an ideology at war with God and his life-giving blueprint for life. Melvin is not being alarmist but he is certainly giving us a wake-up call. He's not being shrill but he's loud—and I'm thankful that he is. That's what I need from an alarm.

It was the economist John Maynard Keynes who

famously noted in *The General Theory of Employment, Interest and Money* that 'practical men who believe themselves to be quite exempt from any intellectual influence, are usually the slaves of some defunct economist. Madmen in authority, who hear voices in the air, are distilling their frenzy from some academic scribbler of a few years back.' The specific rebellious academic scribbles of those associated with the ideology called cultural Marxism have, and continue, to manipulate our culture and prey on its most vulnerable members. Melvin's analysis not only stops us from an unrealistic and overly-optimistic cultural naivety, but also lays out the 'hopeful' ways in which this idolatrous ideology is ultimately toppled by the God who comes down, and by God's people who must challenge this 'Hideous Strength.'

Daniel Strange, BA, PhD,
College Director, Lecturer in Culture,
Religion and Public Theology

Preface

SEVERAL MONTHS AGO, THE STAFF TEAM OF ST JOHN, Newland sat down to watch and discuss a 'Frontline' PBS video entitled *The Persuaders*. This was not the lavish, jaunty 1970's television series recounting the adventures of two debonair international playboys, portrayed by Roger Moore and Tony Curtis; rather, it was a serious exposé of the way marketing gurus shape our desires and tastes through the use of words and images.

It was both fascinating and disturbing.

We were struck by the methods used to sell products that people didn't particularly want. (I am reminded of the cynics definition of advertising as 'the art of getting people to buy what they don't need by describing it in ways they know are not true.') There was no question of presenting reasoned arguments for a product (the last thing you want people to do is *think*); instead, the goal was to capture peoples' *imaginations* through the use of stories and images. Forget the old cliché developed by the US military during the Vietnam War of 'capturing hearts *and* minds,' the target is the heart alone which lies at the root of our desires.

Stories and images are powerful means of getting people to see things in a certain way, as well as representing what is supposed to be 'real'. This is something Robert Joustra and Alissa Wilkinson helpfully explore in their book, *How to Survive the Apocalypse*. By providing a detailed analysis of a dozen or so examples of recent TV series and films, the authors show that the West's view of the future is rather bleak. While earlier generations would craft stories which tended to be optimistic—seeing humankind on an upward climb towards a better and brighter future (think of Gene Rodenberry's *Star Trek*)—that view has now been exchanged for a more dystopian horizon. In the words of Woody Allen, 'The future isn't what it used to be.'

In her review of Joustra and Wilkinson's book, Rachel M. Billings usefully summarises this idea:

> The crumbling 'worlds' these stories depict may be individual lives (as in *Breaking Bad*, *Mad Men*, and *House of Cards*) or global scenarios (as in *Her*, and *The Hunger Games*), projected earthly realities (*The Walking Dead*) or entirely imaginary realms (*Game of Thrones*).

And therefore, Billings goes on to suggest, these programmes reflect a completely human-centred way of thinking, and so not surprisingly the word 'self' frequently appears in the Joustra and Wilkinson's critique of popular culture—in phrases such as 'self-authentication,' 'self-definition,' and 'self-fulfilment.' If everything is relative with no external values, and tradition is passé, what point of reference is there but the self? Billings continues:

> Don Draper of *Mad Men* and Walter White of *Breaking Bad*, for example, both establish themselves as very successful men in some sense—one a heartless advertising executive and the other a ruthless drug lord. But because they have lost sight of any goal outside of their own cravings for power and its attendant privilege, their efforts at becoming 'themselves' end in self-destruction.

There are two points to be made here.

The first is that stories and images are very powerful in portraying what we think the world is like or should be like, and today we are furnished with the means to do this both quickly and widely through modern technology. This is what sociologists refer to as 'connectivity'— we can more or less connect with anyone at anytime, anywhere about anything. More to the point we now have the ability to have access to peoples' imaginations, and so their hearts, in a way which is unparalleled in human history.

The second is the representation of the self as being the 'be all and end all' of human existence. Where has such a thoroughly egocentric understanding come from which is being projected as reality?

This book seeks to show how stories do give insight into the state of affairs in the world and shape how we see the world truly or falsely. It also unpacks the main ideology at work in the West; one which uses technology (especially the media and social networks) and education (or more accurately, propaganda) to promote a thoroughly self-centred understanding of human beings.

We will look at two stories, one from the world of literature, the other from the world of the Scripture, which provide penetrating insights into the spiritual warfare which rages today in the West. The first story, *That Hideous Strength*, was written by C.S. Lewis over 70 years ago. The second story, to which Lewis's fictional work is linked, is the account of the building of the Tower of Babel in Genesis 11. Both will help us understand our times and help formulate a gospel response.

The ideology we shall be exploring is cultural Marxism. This is the machine which drives much of the political correctness which is stifling free thought and speech in our society today, as well as providing the philosophical matrix of much of the gender agenda. I shall argue that this is a 'hideous strength,' a particular manifestation of the principalities and powers seeking to dethrone God and destroy man, and which the story of the Tower of Babel is one of the earliest expressions of a similar corporate rebellion and arrogance which sets itself up against the Creator and his creation.

In the course of this book I shall give some disturbing examples of the way a new totalitarianism is being introduced into Western society and the way the church has colluded with it—at times actively, by buying into cultural Marxism (theological liberalism), or passively, by not concerning itself with such matters so long as one can be left to preach the Word (evangelical pietism). The picture which will be painted will be a bleak one, but, I trust, realistic.

However, the diabolical drama which is being played out in our schools, colleges, work places and government needs to be placed within the bigger biblical drama of God's action in the world through his Son, the Lord Jesus Christ, and his people who are caught up in it, living as strangers and exiles, and called to stand against the world in order to win the world. And so ultimately we can't help but be optimistic which does not preclude entering a new dark age first, as the church has done before.

The words of Rachel Billings in her review of *How to Survive the Apocalypse* is one with which I would agree:

> That's where the Gospel comes in, as I see it; it comes as a power from outside ourselves, interrupting human history and plans. As Christians, we point toward a hope that's far more radical than simply remaining hopeful and acting faithfully. We point toward a new world that God has promised, beyond the nightmares we've created, beyond the dystopias. We point toward our resurrection hope that if we accept Christ's vindication and transformation of us, we have no right to declare our own doom. Because our greatest hope in the midst of this failing world and its institutions is that nothing we can do will save it; only the action of God in Christ, intervening for a second time, can fully redeem and transform this broken creation. So, we wait in hope for a real Apocalypse—the culmination of the Gospel.

I would like to express my appreciation to a number of people who have helped my thinking on these matters, especially Dr Lisa Nolland and Andrew Symes who have helpfully provided material which earthed much of the discussion, and the Revd Tony Jones who has applied his mind to such issues in a local church ministry setting. Thanks also go to Graham Hind and Evangelical Press for their willingness to support this project and last, but by no means least, is my gratitude to my wife Heather whose encouragement never tires.

Melvin Tinker
St John, Newland
Hull
2018
Soli Deo Gloria

Chapter 1
A 2018 Space Trilogy

Introduction

C.S. LEWIS WAS AHEAD OF HIS TIME WHEN HE WROTE THE third of his Space Trilogy, *That Hideous Strength*, back in 1945. John Mark Reynolds claims that it is 'the truest account of the state of the West written in the last one hundred years.' Hyperbole perhaps, but one can't deny Lewis's remarkable prescience in being able to see what was coming down the cultural line. The title itself is taken from a sixteenth-century poem by Sir David Lyndsay called 'Ane Dialog', describing the biblical Tower of Babel as: 'The shadow of that hideous strength / Six miles and more it is of length.' In his preface Lewis wrote, 'This is a "tall story" about devilry, though it has behind it a serious point which I have tried to make in my *Abolition of Man*.'

In *The Abolition of Man* Lewis offered his thoughts on education, the tradition of natural law and the necessity of moral oversight in the sciences. The 'serious point' referred to in the prologue of *That Hideous Strength* entertains the possibility that an intellectual elite of ideologues is capable of changing the way great swathes of a population considers what is 'common sense,' as well as being able to determine which views are permissible, which ideas are passé and, more than that, dangerous. Furthermore, there is the Promethean desire to use science and technology not so much to tame nature but to dominate it to the point of destruction or, as Lewis puts it in *The Abolition of Man*, 'The power of Man to make himself what he pleases means, as we have seen, the power of some men to make other men what they please.'

What Lewis describes by way of fictional narrative is an outlook which derides all that is supernatural and reduces meaning to matter, or, to give it its proper title—naturalistic materialism. This is what Peter Berger describes as 'a world without windows.' No longer do people see the world as a gift (a created order), but they see it as a given (a wholly natural order). In this sense, the secularisation process has produced a revolution that involves what Charles Taylor, calls, the 'social imaginary.' This is not just a set of ideas, but it is 'what enables, through making sense of, the practices of society.'

Lewis was resolutely opposed to what Max Weber termed disenchantment (*entzauberung*), where the magic or mystery of life is not just removed but unwanted and we simply apply reason and technology with the consequence that matters of faith are deemed irrelevant. This modernist outlook is summed up by the social scientist, Philip Rieff, 'What characterises modernity, I think, is just this idea that men need not submit to any power—higher or lower—other than their own.'

When N.I.C.E. is nasty

The bulk of the plot of *That Hideous Strength* concerns the threat of the National Institute of Coordinated Experiments (forming the delicious acronym N.I.C.E.) with its aim to free humanity from nature. The symbol adopted by N.I.C.E., which is devoted to 'Technocratic and Objective Man,' was a muscular male nude grasping a thunderbolt. The overall goal of the organisation is 'the scientific reconstruction of the human race in the direction of increased efficiency.' The irony is that while the group eschews all that is supernatural— embracing a purely materialistic view of reality—Lewis portrays it as being under the direction of unseen, sinister spiritual forces, what he called '[dark] eldilic energy and [dark] eldilic knowledge.' Lewis uses the term 'macrobes' for the demonic powers hovering from above, 'The structure of the macrobe, so far as we know it, is of extreme simplicity. When I say that it is above the animal level, I mean that it is more permanent, disposes more energy, and has greater intelligence.' These are the 'rulers,' 'authorities,' and 'spiritual forces of evil in the heavenly places' of which the apostle Paul speaks in Ephesians 6:12.

The main image of evil in the story is Alcasan's Head, the forerunner of 'a new species—the Chosen Heads who never die,' separated from its body and kept alive artificially. In his helpful critique of the story, Pete

Lowman suggests the various meanings associated with this figure:

> This image is given multiple, related meanings. Firstly, it stands for the rational processes operating in supposedly 'objective' separation from the moral law. As Lewis says in the 1955 Preface, he is making the same point here as he did in his essay *The Abolition of Man*; and in the latter book he describes thinkers who move in that direction as 'men without chests ... The head rules the belly through the chest—the seat ... of emotions organized by trained habit into stable sentiments.' Secondly, Lewis is using the amputated Head to stand for a rationalism that cuts itself adrift from or is hostile to 'Nature'. And a third variant appears when N.I.C.E initiate, Frost, compares humanity to an animal no longer needing a large body for nutrition and locomotive organs: 'The masses are therefore to disappear. The body is to become all head. The human race is to become all Technocracy'—and so sixteen major wars are scheduled for the twentieth century.

Lewis is not at all unabashed in bringing the supernatural to the fore at various points throughout the story, but in doing this he drew his strongest criticism. In one early review, George Orwell wrote, 'One could recommend this book unreservedly if Mr. Lewis had succeeded in keeping it all on a single level. Unfortunately, the supernatural keeps breaking in, and it does so in rather confusing, undisciplined ways.' More recently, Rowan Williams has written of the destruction of the evil characters at the end of the story in the following way:

'Over the top,' I think, is the only expression one can use for this. I think it's when the elephant breaks loose and comes into the dining room and begins trampling people to death that I feel something has snapped in the authorial psyche.

However, this approach was quite intentional by Lewis, as he made clear in a letter to Dorothy L. Sayers written after receiving several negative reviews. 'Apparently reviewers will not tolerate a mixture of the realistic and the supernatural. Which is a pity, because (a) it's just the mixture I like, and (b) we have to put up with it in real life.'

> *If it is the case that we are involved in a spiritual battle Christians can't yield the field to the secularists*

If it is the case that we are involved in a spiritual battle, as the Bible makes clear, Christians can't yield the field to the secularists, in fact they have all the more vigorously to assert the supernatural for, as we shall see in due course, whatever the particular ideologies the church has to contend with, they are manifestations of forces which mere human means are unable to overcome. As Paul makes clear in 2 Corinthians 10:3–5:

> For though we walk in the flesh, we are not waging war according to the flesh. For the weapons of our warfare are not of the flesh but have divine power to destroy

strongholds. We destroy arguments and every lofty opinion raised against the knowledge of God.

Lewis was simply following the apostle Paul at this point.

Science vs. scientism

The way in which the members of N.I.C.E. seek to realise the organisation's aims is primarily through education but they also employ technology. Lewis knows that ideas never remain hermetically sealed within the academy, they eventually flow out to shape society and more importantly influence *individual* human beings for good or ill. Such individuals are represented in the story by the newly married Studdocks. In an edition of *Punch* published in August 1945, H. P. Edens wrote, 'it is Mr Lewis's triumph to have shown, with shattering credibility, how the pitiful little souls of Jane and Mark Studdock become the apocalyptic battlefield of Heaven.'

Lewis's critique was not universally well received at the time. Some, like the humanistic scientist, J.B.S. Haldane, were particularly offended. Replying to Haldane's concerns, Lewis said that scientists *per se* were not his target, but rather certain *trends* which were beginning to creep into society such as 'officials' using the power of a small group to subvert (the 'inner ring'), the exaltation of the collective with little concern for the individual, the 'Party' that obeys an impersonal force and believes in human progress using whatever means necessary to bring about the 'liberation' of people, especially those who do not yet realise they need liberating; and the way education in particular was being invaded by naturalistic and anti-religious indoctrination.

This may well be, but there is little doubt that it was *scientism*—a wholesale philosophical movement which, as a matter of principle (not evidence), has no room for God—as specifically represented by the likes of Haldane that Lewis had in his sights and so Haldane had every reason to take it personally. Haldane was a leading proponent of what became known as 'social Darwinism', ideas that are most clearly exposited in his essay 'Eugenics and Social Reform'. He proposed the optimisation of the human gene pool by preventing certain types of people from breeding. This was an idea also championed by Bertrand Russell who, in 1929, advocated the compulsory sterilisation of the mentally deficient. Russell argued that the state should have the power to forcibly sterilise all those regarded as mentally deficient by appropriate experts and, he argued, the resulting reduction of 'idiots, imbeciles and feeble minded' people would be of such a benefit to society that it would outweigh any dangers of misuse. Lewis saw the need to challenge such views, hence he wrote *That Hideous Strength*.

Nothing buttery

Lewis was accurate in describing the zeitgeist which was to move so powerfully throughout the post-war West. I studied biological sciences at university in the 1970's and without doubt the naturalistic materialism of the likes of Jacques Monod, Francis Crick and B.F. Skinner, with their reductionistic understanding of humans as being 'nothing but a bundle of neurological reflexes', was all the rage. The philosophical label which was attached to this approach was 'ontological reductionism.' As early as the 1950's Professor D.M. MacKay dubbed this standpoint 'nothing buttery,' which he showed to be philosophically bankrupt. The offence this position is to plain common sense is ably illustrated by the story of B.F. Skinner's visit to Keele University to give a lecture. After Skinner had delivered the formal lecture, in which he emphasised an objective, mechanistic description as a *total* explanation of man's behaviour, he was invited to have an informal discussion with Professor McKay who had chaired the meeting. Skinner was asked whether in fact he was interested at all in who he, the chairman, and others were. Skinner simply replied, 'I am interested in the noises coming from your mouth!' Such reductionism is still doing the rounds as we see from this bold assertion by Richard Dawkins:

> We are machines built by DNA whose purpose is to make more copies of the same DNA ... Flowers are for the same thing as everything else in the living kingdoms, for spreading 'copy me' programmes about, written in DNA language. That is EXACTLY what we are for. We are machines for propagating DNA, and the propagation of DNA is self-sustaining process. It is every living objects sole reason for living.

Lewis certainly *was* ahead of his time!

Babies and bathwaters

However, it is perhaps worth pointing out that in his zeal to alert the unsuspecting world to the dangers of naturalist materialism, Lewis may have overstepped the mark and so weakened his apologetic—throwing out the proverbial baby with the proverbial bathwater.

In *The Abolition of Man* Lewis mounts a protest against 'Baconian technology,' claiming that both magic and applied science share a common ground in that they both try to subdue reality to the wishes of man. He condemned human dominion over nature as being hubris and praised the ancient wisdom of conforming to nature. But this is more of a Stoic understanding, not a biblical one. For whatever reason, Lewis did not offer biblical support for his position. A more measured and biblical understanding is offered by Professor Reijer Hooykaas:

> It is true that the results of our dominion over nature have been unhealthy in many cases; the powerful river of modern science and technology has often caused disastrous inundations. But by comparison the contemplative, almost mediaeval vision that is offered as an alternative would be a stagnant pool.

However, Lewis's antipathy towards modern technology and perhaps a less than biblical understanding of nature, does not detract from some of his main points which have tremendous significance for us today, namely, the desire of humans to define reality (for example what it means to be human), the use of technology and education (propaganda) to achieve a re-visioning of the way things are, the power of a few ideologues using modern means to influence the many and the underlying spiritual battle which belies these things.

The times they are a changin'

We have purposely spent some time looking at how Lewis foresaw the menace that results from a purely materialistic understanding of humanity. This not only helps us understand more fully the purpose and plot of Lewis's book, but gives a concrete example of what happens when humans surrender to another power other than God. But that was then, and this is now. In the relatively short span of 50 years the intellectual and cultural landscape of the West has morphed into something the scientists of Lewis's day, and those who have followed in their wake, could hardly have imagined; although in some ways they did prepare the way, not least by making Christianity appear to be an unviable intellectual option in the late-twentieth century.

> *The 'hideous strength' is very much at work today and needs to be confronted by the church*

The 'hideous strength' which Lewis described so imaginatively, and which the Tower of Babel embodies so eloquently, is very much at work today and needs to be confronted by the church with every fibre of its being. Whilst not closing our eyes to the vestiges and dangers of scientism which still lingers at least in the popular consciousness, there is a new manifestation of that 'hideous strength' every much as powerful and dangerous as that which Lewis described, exhibiting the same characteristics and aims. The recent reminder by Kevin J. Vanhoozer is timely, 'For we wrestle not against flesh and blood, matters in motion, but against *isms*, against the powers that seek to name, and control, reality.'

Man-made religion

Lewis's reference to the Tower of Babel is pregnant with significance.

In the epigraph of *That Hideous Strength*, Lewis makes it clear that he sees the aims of N.I.C.E. as a comparable instance of human power extending beyond 'that limitation ... which mercy had imposed ... as a protection.' As we shall see, the Tower of Babel was not simply a *human* project; it was fundamentally a *religious* enterprise. It has often been said that Marxism is a corruption of the Christian faith—having its own prophet (Marx), Bible (*Das Kapital*), gospel (dialectical materialism), apostles (Lenin, Trotsky) and eschatology (the overthrow of capitalism and the establishment of the worker's ideal). Similarly in Lewis's novel, while the progressives disavow traditional Christianity, the language used and the zeal displayed to bring about a new world order are decidedly religious in nature. This is why Lewis has one of the main characters, the Revd Straik, present the new science in religious terms:

> The Kingdom of God is to be realised here—in this world. And it will be. At the name of Jesus every knee shall bow. In that name I dissociate myself completely from all the organised religion that has yet been seen in the world … Therefore, where we see power, we see the sign of His coming, and that is why I find myself joining with communists and materialists and anyone else who is ready to expedite the coming. The feeblest of these people here has the tragic sense of life, the ruthlessness, the total commitment, the readiness to sacrifice all merely human values, which I could not find amid all the nauseating cant of the organised religions.

The 'hideous strength' which is exerting itself in Western society and the Western church today exhibits all the characteristics that the members of N.I.C.E. just described, and it is also comparable to the Tower of Babel. To this end, I want to use the story recorded in Genesis 11 as a parabolic lens through which we can view and come to understand what has been happening in our society and how it may be countered by the gospel of Jesus Christ.

First, we must polish up the lens and go back to Babel.

Chapter 2
The Rabble at Babel

A PHRASE COINED BY C.S. LEWIS AND HIS FRIEND OWEN Barfield which has now become well known is 'chronological snobbery.' This refers to the widely held view that whatever belonged to an earlier time is inferior to the present simply by virtue of its temporal location. It is captured by the saying, 'trad is bad and the latest is the greatest.' However, there is often much value in looking at something from a different age as it may offer a corrective to our own prejudices and limited perspectives. When we come to the account in Genesis 11 of the building of the Tower of Babel, early church commentators had some interesting insights. In his

There is value in looking at something from a different age as it may offer a corrective to our own prejudices

discussion of the biblical narrative, James Austin provides this helpful summary:

'The men who migrate from the east in order to found Babylon are led by ambition and pride' (Chrysostom). 'Babylon is founded by Nimrod, as the capital of his kingdom. The inhabitants of Babylon construct the tower because in their pride they want to defy the power of God' (Augustine). 'The inhabitants of Babylon are giants who built the tower for their own salvation' (Pseudo-Dionysius). 'When God says, "Come, let us go down and there confuse their language," he is addressing the other persons of the Trinity' (Augustine). 'The Son is the one who is sent to the earth in order to confuse the language' (Novatian). 'Since the inhabitants of Babylon use the privilege of having a single language for evil purposes, God confuses their speech so that they are not able to understand each other anymore' (Chrysostom). 'God sees that they are able to build the tower because they speak the same language. Therefore, he confuses their language in order to prevent them from finishing their building' (Commodian).

While this summary provides a mix of astute observation and fanciful speculation, the main theological points are sound and grounded in the Biblical text of Genesis 11:1–9:

Now the whole earth had one language and the same words. And as people migrated from the east, they found a plain in the land of Shinar and settled there. And they said to one another, 'Come, let us make bricks, and burn them thoroughly.' And they had brick for stone, and bitumen for mortar. Then they said, 'Come, let us build ourselves a city and a tower with its top in the heavens, and let us make a name for ourselves, lest we be dispersed over the face of the whole earth.' And the LORD came down to see the city and the tower, which the children of man had built. And the LORD said, 'Behold, they are one people, and they have all one language, and this is only the beginning of what they will do. And nothing that they propose to do will now be impossible for them. Come, let us go down and there confuse their language, so that they may not understand one another's speech.' So the LORD dispersed them from there over the face of all the earth, and they left off building the city. Therefore its name was called Babel, because there the LORD confused the language of all the earth. And from there the LORD dispersed them over the face of all the earth.

United we stand

God's cultural mandate to 'fill the earth and subdue it' is given to human beings in Genesis 1:28 and reiterated to Noah in Genesis 9:7. This is roundly repudiated by the peoples of the earth in Genesis 11:4 as they decide to settle on the plain of Shinar to build a tower so that they would *not* be scattered over the globe.

There is a decidedly universal feel to what is happening. The word 'all' or 'whole' (Hebrew *kul*) appears at a number of points in the narrative. In verse 1, the 'whole earth' is the description of the scope of humanity; whereas, verses 4 and 8 describe the whole earth into which humanity would be distributed. The whole of humanity is referred to in verse 9 and mentioned again earlier in verse 6 relating to the sharing of a common language.

In other words, this is an exercise of collective rebellion. Austin writes, 'The compiler seemed determined to communicate that all of the people of this period were involved as "one" people, a concept that agrees with Genesis' emphasis on the universality of sin.'

The peoples display great technological ingenuity in the building of the tower with bricks utilising the materials of their environment to create something as strong as stone, but malleable like clay. Cain may have built a city in Genesis 4:17, but that was nothing compared to this latest enterprise. Since then humankind has advanced, it appears to be in a position to shape nature rather than be shaped by nature. People can 'boldly go where no man has been before' to use the words of the gospel according to Gene Rodenberry in the 1960's Star Trek series. There is now a tower in this city which people can see for miles and stand gazing at in amazement.

> *The Tower of Babel is an exercise of collective rebellion*

For the fame of our name

We are told that the primary motivation in their attempt was to make a 'name for themselves.' This forces us to ask: How could such a name be gained? The answer lies in what it is hoped the tower will achieve. Contrary to the common view that the Ziggurat was a means by which *humans* might *ascend* to the heights of heaven, it was seen as a holy place which would bring *God down* from heaven. The assumption is that with the right technique and 'expertise' humankind can domesticate God, enticing him down to dwell among them and so bless them. In the pagan mind it was based on the belief that the gods had needs which humans could meet and as such the Babel account represents a distortion of the nature of God, corrupting his image by reshaping him in *their* image. Having the power to 'bring God down,' in more senses than one, is bound to result in a great name, for you then appear greater than God himself!

Symptoms of sin

Here we have testimony to human ingenuity and determination which in this instance, as John Piper argues in *Spectacular Sins*, are outward expressions of two inward sins.

> *Babel represents a distortion of the nature of God, reshaping him in their image*

The first sin is the craving for human praise. This doesn't mean it is wrong to praise people. When something has been achieved which is laudable, we should give people their due recognition. But it is when we live for human praise, and when human praise becomes the force which motivates us that it turns into a form of idolatry.

The second sin is to do with the craving for security—hence the desire to build the city so that people aren't dispersed. There is nothing wrong in seeking praise or security in themselves, what matters is from *whom* we seek ultimate praise and security. What we have in this account is a society which wants both of those things without God.

Also note the importance language plays. The people see language as a means of *power* to *do* things, not just to *talk about* things. The three fold, 'let us' spoken by humans, mimics God's creative act in making humans in Genesis 1:26. And it is this power of the use of language which God disrupts in an act of judgment and mercy as he 'comes down' by his own volition in verse 5. There is judgment which results in the inability to exercise such power with Promethean pride as God confuses their languages; but also mercy by God's limitation of that power which, because of the wickedness of the human heart, would invariably be abused. Ironically, what was designed to bring fame becomes a symbol of folly.

But there is another element of defiance which might be in operation.

Blurring the boundaries

In the creation account of Genesis 1 God brings order out of chaos by the twofold act of 'separation' (establishing boundaries) and 'filling': the separation of light from darkness; water from water, land from sky and the attendant filling: fish, vegetation, animals, heavenly bodies and birds, each suited to its own sphere:

The earth was

shapeless   empty

Day 1
The separation of
Light and darkness.

Day 4
Creation of lights to
rule the day and night.

Day 2
Separation of waters
Form sky and sea.

Day 5
Creation of birds and
fish to fill Sky and sea.

Day 3
Separation of the sea
From the dry land and
the creation of plants.

Day 6
Creation of animals and
humans to fill the land
and eat the plants.

Day 7
The heavens and the earth were finished and God rested.

In the narrative of Noah and the flood in Genesis 7 we see those boundaries removed so the world collapses back into a kind of primeval chaos.

The importance of things occupying their rightful place within the bounds *God* has decreed is underscored by the purity laws in Leviticus 11 where the animals are rendered clean according to where they occupy the threefold division of Genesis 1—above, below or dry land—as distinct from the animals which are unclean by virtue of the fact they somehow blur those boundaries (e.g. animals in the water which do *not* have fins or scales). Far from these laws being arbitrary, they are meant to be daily reminders to God's people that it is *God* who is creator not man; *he* determines the nature of reality, not us. The laws against homosexuality, transvestism and bestiality also stand against such destructive blurring and deconstructing of the boundaries of creation. Could it therefore not be that by building the tower from the *earth* to the *heavens*, that the peoples in Genesis 11 are transgressing in much the say way in their attempt to redefine God?

The three 'Cs'

There are three ways that the 'hideous strength' attempts to exert itself over and against God which this episode illustrates.

> *These laws are not arbitrary, they remind God's people that God determines the nature of reality, not man*

First, there is *communalism*—the group identity and solidarity in rebellion. While the rest of the Genesis' narratives have individuals who are identified as playing significant roles, here we have humankind as a group acting to the detriment of the individual.

Second, there is *constructionism,* literally in the building of a city and a tower, but also in using language to reshape reality, believing and declaring that we are able to bring God down and so de-god God, who is the ultimate reality. It is then a short step from this idolatrous construal to reimagining everything else—which of course the pagan world did by identifying different parts of creation as gods which needed somehow to be controlled.

Thirdly, there is *connectivity*. Being in one place and having one language enables the people to connect with each other and so perpetuate their blasphemous ideas and actions even further.

What we have in the Tower of Babel episode is in effect a *rival cosmology* to that of God's; it is an unmaking and a remaking of the world, a blasphemous human 'let us' over and against the Holy 'let us' of the Triune God.

Chapter 3
What goes round comes around

LET US NOW TAKE A LOOK AT HOW THE 'HIDEOUS strength' has been increasing its grip in the West.

From 'was-isms' to 'now-isms'

We saw how for Lewis, the ideology of his day, which he sought to expose and debunk, was naturalistic materialism. One of the main ideologies of our day is a variant of this, namely, neo-Marxism, sometimes called cultural Marxism or libertarian Marxism.

One of its modern advocates, Sydney Hook, defines it as:

> A philosophy of human liberation. It seeks to overcome human alienation, to emancipate man from repressive social institutions, especially economic institutions that

frustrate his true nature, and to bring him into harmony with himself, his fellow men, and the world around him so that he can overcome his estrangements and express his true essence through creative freedom.

(Remember how in Lewis's story it is one of the aims of N.I.C.E. to liberate men from nature?)

But the liberty which the cultural Marxists have in mind is not the liberty of classical liberalism—equality under the law or even equality of opportunity. Unlike the classical Marxist whose main focus was economic inequality, theirs is an equality cutting across the *whole* of human experience. It was Herbert Marcuse of the Frankfurt School who argued that traditional societies promote what he called a 'repressive tolerance' because they do not deal with the latent inequalities of humans; the fact that some are cleverer, wiser or harder working than others, who are then to be considered to be oppressed because of their perceived deficiency. As Andrew Sandlin writes:

> Libertarian Marxism is all about liberating humanity from the social institutions and conditions (like the family and church and business and traditional views and habits and authorities) that prevent the individual from realizing his true self, his true desires and aspirations, from being anything he wants to be—full autonomy … Libertarian Marxism is the Marxism of our culture, of our time.

How is such a revolution—one in which 'God

is brought down,' and his objective creation to which humanity must conform is discredited—to be achieved?

Here we come to the writings of the Italian Marxist Antonio Gramsci and his key idea of 'hegemony' (from the Greek *hegemon*, which means 'ruler'). This is the process by which a dominant class (think of the directors of N.I.C.E. in Lewis's story) exerts and maintains its influence over people through noncoercive means such as schools, the media and marketing. It works by changing what Peter Berger calls the 'plausibility structures' of a society, that is those background assumptions, beliefs and ways of thinking and acting which are taken as given. It is the presumption which declares 'Of course, everyone now days knows that …' The aim is to get people to think and *feel* for themselves that certain values and practices, such as same-sex marriage, are common sense, fair or even natural.

Over the last 60 years or so in the West there has effectively occurred the death of one culture, rooted in the Judeo-Christian world view, and the rise of another more secular one. Philip Rieff observes that, 'The death of a culture begins when its normative institutions fail to communicate ideals in ways that remain *inwardly* compelling.' Once the ideology of neo-Marxism becomes 'inwardly compelling' (although you don't scare the horses by *calling* it neo-Marxism, you talk instead about 'equality,' 'liberation' and 'tolerance'—the things of which the Church of England speaks endlessly) the revolution is more or less complete. The upshot of this is that if *these* beliefs and practices are considered plausible, *Christian* beliefs and practices become implausible more or less by default, in which case it will not do simply to *argue* for the cogency of the Christian faith for most people will think that there is nothing to argue *about*. Many of us don't spend that much time thinking how we might argue against flat earthists—we simply assume they are mistaken, out of touch and an irrelevance; so it is with many people's view of Christianity.

One of the key tools for achieving such a change of perception and feeling is by the destabilisation of language, thus enabling a new language to be devised by which the power of the elite can be exerted. The goal for Marcuse was to, 'break the established universe of meaning.' This lies at the heart of social constructionism (words do not

The result is that if secular beliefs and practices become plausible, Christian beliefs become implausible by default

necessarily *refer* to anything, except perhaps to other words in a language matrix) but they are *tools*, units of power to be employed deconstructing and reconstructing, creating our own Tower of Babel around which we can rally and 'bring God down.' This involves censoring not just words but *thoughts,* and it is here that the 'hideous strength' is seen at its strongest. According to Marcuse, cultural subversion 'must begin with stopping the words and images which feed this [opposing] consciousness. To be sure, this is censorship, even pre-censorship'. He writes:

Tolerance cannot be indiscriminate and equal with respect to the contents of expression, neither in word nor in deed; it cannot protect false words and wrong deeds which demonstrate that they contradict and counteract the possibilities of liberation. Such indiscriminate tolerance is justified in harmless debates, in conversation, in academic discussion; it is indispensable in the scientific enterprise, in private religion. But society cannot be indiscriminate where the pacification of existence, where freedom and happiness themselves are at stake: here, certain things *cannot* be said, certain ideas *cannot* be expressed, certain policies *cannot* be proposed, certain behaviour *cannot* be permitted without making tolerance an instrument for the continuation of servitude. [emphasis mine]

Notice all those 'cannots'? Who do you think they are applied to? Mainly people like Christians. This is a new totalitarian-tolerance while all the time masquerading as a new freedom. As such the new tolerance must extinguish the old tolerance and those people and institutions which traditionally espouse it such as the church. Furthermore, for neo-Marxism to have a *raison d'être* there must be repressed groups which need liberating. People are required to see themselves as *victims* of the liberal society of which they are a part.

PC or not PC? That is the question

It is cultural Marxism which lies behind the all-pervading political correctness of our age. Those of both the political right and left acknowledge this. Pat Buchanan of the right wrote, 'Political Correctness is cultural Marxism, a regime to punish dissent and to stigmatize social heresy as the Inquisition punished religious heresy. Its trademark is intolerance.' Similarly from the more liberal publication *Newsweek*:

> PC is, strictly speaking, a totalitarian philosophy … Politically, PC is Marxist in origin … There are … some who recognize the tyranny of PC but see it only as a transitional phase, which will no longer be necessary once the virtues of tolerance are internalized. Does that sound familiar? It's the dictatorship of the proletariat.

There are two notable and concerning features regarding the ideology of political correctness.

First of all there is the assigning of value to people according to their group identity, defined according to broad sociological categories like race, gender, sexual orientation and so on. But such categories are not comparable. Race, such as being ethnically black, is not the same as ideology, such as feminism. Some may consider homosexuality to be a lifestyle choice, others a moral issue, both of which are very different matters to race and ideology. Furthermore, what is one to do with the mixing of categories, such as being a black, feminist homosexual? Is one's value as an oppressed minority tripled compared to someone who simply falls into a single category? Is it not also condescending to have, say, a black woman as a token representative of a group simply because of her race and gender, for does this not suggest that 'all black women are the same'?

In the second place truth is at a discount. As we have noted with Marcuse, certain truths are to be declared none-truths, subject to social or even state censorship because they hurt people's feelings or are considered intolerant. This means that some groups and individuals are immune from criticism. The parallels with overt totalitarian regimes are striking.

Critical Theory and the Frankfurt School

In 1923 a week-long symposium was organised by Felix Weil in Frankfurt, Germany in which they laid out a vision for a Marxist think-tank and research centre. The original name for the centre was the Institute for Marxism (*Institut fur Marxismus*), but a more innocent sounding title was subsequently given, The Institute for Social Research (*Institut fur Sozialforschung*). Since that time the ISR has usually been known simply as the Frankfurt School.

In 1930 Max Horkheimer became the director of the ISR which is when neo-Marxism was launched in earnest. Horkheimer was convinced that the major obstacle to the spread of Marxism was traditional Western culture with its Judeo-Christian heritage. Here there developed a revisionist neo-Marxist interpretation of Western culture under the rubric, Critical Theory, the goal of which according to William S. Lind 'was not truth but praxis, or revolutionary action: bringing the current society and culture down through unremitting, destructive criticism.' Truth, according to this view, was locked into its own particular point in history and so was historically relative (of course that would apply to Critical Theory itself a fact which was conveniently overlooked).

Weapons of mass deception

A key element of Critical Theory was the integration of Marxism with Darwinism and Freudianism. Drawing in Freudianism was quite a bold move for the Frankfurt School since according Breshears:

> Philosophically, Freudianism was inherently counterrevolutionary in that it discounted the primacy of economics in human social evolution in favour of liberation through psychoanalysis and the release of libidinal impulses. Rather than a violent external revolution that immediately liberated the masses, the Freudian revolution was peaceful, deliberative, individual and internal.

Nonetheless, great potential was seen in harnessing Freudianism for their cause. According to Horkheimer and his fellow scholars, bourgeois society is inherently sexually repressed, which is a major factor in neurosis and other forms of mental illness. 'They believed,' as Breshears makes clear, 'that a revolutionary, post-capitalist and post-Christian society could liberate humanity from this repression, so sexual liberation from the restrictions of a patriarchal society was a major theme in their ideology.'

Both Eric Fromm and Wilhelm Reich re-worked Freudianism into the neo-Marxist ideology. Fromm argued that sexual orientation is merely a social construct, that there are no innate differences between men and women, and furthermore that sexuality and gender roles are socially determined. It was Reich who coined the term 'the sexual revolution' (the title of his 1936 book) and contended that the innate sexual impulse should be liberated from artificial and man-made moral restrictions.

But perhaps more than any other member of the Frankfurt School it was Herbert Marcuse who was to have the most far-reaching influence in this aspect of the neo-Marxist ideology. In *Eros and Civilization* he sought to bring together neo-Marxism with a version of neo-Freudianism in order to turn the power of the libido into a revolutionary force. He called for the throwing off of all traditional values and sexual restraints in favour of 'polymorphous perversity.' The very idea of marital love and fidelity was considered by Marcuse to be counter-revolutionary. Although cultural change was the ultimate goal, Marcuse understood the tactical appeal of the pleasure principle. For as we are often reminded, 'sex sells,' and it sells politics too, what better way to recruit revolutionaries than to convince them that sexual promiscuity is a sure way to bring about the revolution? Dinesh D'Souza notes in *What's so great about Christianity?* the centrality of this tactic by quoting a neo-Marxist, 'Against the power of religion we employ an equal if not greater power—the power of hormones.'

In for the long haul

For the members of the Frankfurt School, accomplishing

such a revolution would involve infiltrating the key institutions, not least the educational establishments (the parallels with N.I.C.E. are self-evident as it occupies the grounds within an old university). It was assumed that there would be a commitment to the long term, or 'the long march through the institutions'—a reference to Mao Zedong's Long March to eventual victory in the Chinese Civil War.

This is how Breshears describes the different stages in the long march as it worked itself out in the United States:

Throughout the 1960s, with the escalation of the Vietnam War, many college and university graduates enrolled in master's programs in hopes of evading the draft, and some of the most radical eventually earned Ph.D.s with the intention of fundamentally transforming American society through the education system. (Of all the Ph.D. degrees granted by American universities in the 110 years between 1860 and 1970, half were granted in the 1960s.) Others opted to avoid the draft by enrolling in seminary and becoming ministers in liberal Protestant denominations or priests in the Roman Catholic Church. By the mid-to-late 1970s many of these former student radicals were moving into positions as junior faculty and administrators, and by the early 1980s they were firmly entrenched in most universities and attaining tenure. Gradually, liberal arts faculties became more radical as Neo-Marxists began replacing older New Deal liberals who retired, and over time a rigid left-wing ideology prevailed in many departments ... Likewise, just as former Sixties activists came to dominate in higher education, they moved into key positions of influence in the mainstream media—radio, television, and print media. As their cultural influence and power increased over time, they grew bolder and more aggressive.

One would venture to suggest a similar progression in the United Kingdom.

If you don't agree it is because you are a fascist

By a semantic sleight of hand, those who appear critical of the neo-Marxist agenda are labelled fascist, a move originally made in 1950 by Theodor Adorno in his book, *The Authoritarian Personality.*

Adorno constructed an *F-scale* (Fascist-Scale), a rating system based on nine personality variables. These are the following traits:

1. Conventionalism. Rigid adherence to conventional middle-class values.

2. Authoritarian submission. A submissive and uncritical attitude toward authority figures.

3. Authoritarian aggression. The inclination to apply or enforce conventional values on others.

4. Anti-intraception. Opposition to the subjective, the imaginative, or the intuitive.

5. Superstition and stereotypy. The belief in the supernatural or mystical determinism, and the

disposition to think in rigid categories (i.e. racial, ethnic and gender prejudice).

6. Power and toughness. A preoccupation with dominance-submission, strong-weak, leader follower; identification with power figures; exaggerated assertion of strength and toughness.

7. Destructiveness and cynicism. Generalised hostility and the tendency to vilify others.

8. Projectivity. 'The disposition to believe that wild and dangerous things go on in the world.'

9. Sex. An exaggerated concern with conventional sexual morality and a preoccupation with other people's sexual practices.

This is a tactical definition which immediately puts Christians in their place as die hard fascists! It would be tempting to play Adorno at his own game and produce an *M-scale* by simply modifying the above traits in a different direction (e.g. Unconventionlism. A childish and unthinking adherence to the latest popular trend. Authoritarian aggression. The inclination to apply or enforce unconventional values on others), but this achieves very little except to expose the fallacious logic and propagandistic nature of the neo-Marxist enterprise.

Bulverism for today

What this affords is an example of what C.S. Lewis dubbed 'Bulverism' whereby an opponent's belief is assumed to be wrong and credited as being the result of some bias and thus can be discounted once it has been discredited. The reasons for an opponent's position do not then need to be considered. In fact it is to neo-Marxism's advantage that one does not draw people's attention to reasons, for then their own position might be examined and found wanting while the alternative position is found strong and compelling.

This is how Lewis describes what happens:

The Freudians have discovered that we exist as bundles of complexes ... Nowadays the Freudian will tell you to go and analyse the hundred: you will find that they all think Elizabeth [I] a great queen because they all have a mother-complex. Their thoughts are psychologically tainted at the source ... Now this is obviously great fun; but it has not always been noticed that there is a bill to pay for it. There are two questions that people who say this kind of thing ought to be asked. The first is, are all thoughts thus tainted at the source, or only some? The second is, does the taint invalidate the tainted thought—in the sense of making it untrue—or not? If they say that all thoughts are thus tainted, then, of course, we must remind them that Freudianism and Marxism are as much systems of thought as Christian theology ... The Freudian and Marxian are in the same boat with all the rest of us, and cannot criticize us from outside. They have sawn off the branch they were sitting on. If, on the other hand, they say that the taint need not invalidate their thinking, then neither need it invalidate ours. In which case they have saved their own branch, but also saved ours along with it.

This is now a standard tactic used against those who oppose cultural Marxism and the various sub ideologies it has spawned. Forget argument and reason, assume your opponent is just wrong or stupid (or both) and explain his ideas away by appealing to pseudoscience. This happened to me a few years ago when I was in Jerusalem at the Global Anglican Future Conference (GAFCON). During the conference there was a large gay pride event taking place down the road from where we were meeting and I was invited by the BBC to attend and debate with one of its leaders. The interview appeared on BBC world news. As you can imagine I received a fair bit of correspondence as a result, and not all of it was favourable! One of the most interesting letters I received was from someone who was gay saying that my objection to homosexual practice must be because *I* was repressing a latent homosexuality of my own. This is pure Bulverism. He could not or didn't want to concede that I might have reasons to think that homosexual practice was wrong and stands as an example of disordered sexuality—so there must be some psychological explanation for my position, namely, I must be gay but refusing to acknowledge it.

A new Dark Age?

Michael Minnicino assesses the impact of the Frankfurt School over the past seventy-five years and offers a possible solution to reverse the damage that has been done to

Western culture. He warns if America and the West continue down the road to self-destruction, it could very well usher in a dreadful new Dark Age in human history:

> The principles through which Western Judeo-Christian civilization was built, are now no longer dominant in our society; they exist only as a kind of underground resistance movement. If that resistance is ultimately submerged, then the civilization will not survive—and in our era of pandemic disease and nuclear weapons, the collapse of Western civilization will very likely take the rest of the world with it to Hell. The way out is to create a Renaissance. If that sounds grandiose, it is nonetheless what is needed. A renaissance means, to start again: to discard the evil, inhuman, and just plain stupid, and to go back hundreds or thousands of years to the ideas which allow humanity to grow in freedom and goodness. Once we have identified those core beliefs, we can start to rebuild civilization.

Talk of a renaissance might grate with some Christians; surely it would be better to speak of reformation or revival? Os Guinness makes a reasoned plea for the use of the phrase. He argues for a Christian renaissance, pointing out that the term 'is simply the French word for rebirth, and its deepest roots—and fulfilment—all the way back to Jesus himself and to his night-time conversation with Nicodemus. Rebirth is essentially a Christian notion.' He goes on:

> But the term itself is not what matters ... what matters is that it is a movement led by the Spirit of God, which

involves God's people returning to the ways of God and so demonstrating in our time the kingdom of God, and not in word only but in power and with the plausibility of community expression.

What this might look like will be taken up in a later chapter. Suffice to say that the 'hideous strength' is abroad and the church needs to wake up to the fact as the darkness begins to draw in even closer.

Reimagining the world

As we have seen, by their actions the people of Babel revealed their view of God, the world and how God was supposed to relate to the world (what we might call their cosmology) which was at variance with Genesis 1 and 2. Similarly today godless views of humanity and the world are being constructed (even within the church) which are diametrically opposed both to God's general and special revelation. Perhaps nowhere is this seen most sharply than in the area of the gay and transgender debate.

> *The 'hideous strength' is abroad and the church needs to wake up as the darkness draws closer*

Chapter 4
The Gender agenda

THE UNDERLYING NATURE OF THE PRESENT CLASH between the Judeo-Christian world view and the dominant secularist view in the West is underscored by Rod Dreher's subtitle to his article, 'Sex After Christianity: Gay marriage is not just a social revolution but a cosmological one'.

Dreher draws attention to a cover story in a 1993 copy of *The Nation*, which said that if the gay-rights cause wanted to succeed, it would have to design 'a complete cosmology.' As Dreher puts it, 'the gay-rights cause has succeeded precisely because the Christian cosmology has dissipated in the mind of the West.' Summarising this 'new' cosmology, he writes, 'To be modern is to believe in one's individual desires as the locus of authority and self-definition.' Dreher points out that Christians have tended to approach the issue of homosexuality as a moral issue (which it is) but have failed to see it as a cosmological issue, a redefining and reconfiguring of reality—a new Babel.

Having a ball?

The employment of Gramscian strategy is very much in evidence in Marshall Kirk and Hunter Madsen's *After the Ball: How America Will Conquer its Fear and Hatred of Gays in the 90s*. Al Mohler writes:

> The spectacular success of the homosexual movement stands as one of the most fascinating phenomena of our time. In less than two decades, homosexuality has moved from 'the love that dares not speak its name,' to the centre of America's public life. The homosexual agenda has advanced even more quickly than its most ardent proponents had expected, and social change of this magnitude demands some explanation.

He rightly draws attention to the influence of this book as providing part of the answer.

Kirk and Madsen (both Harvard graduates and 'Madmen'—Maddison Avenue advertising consultants) combined psychiatric and public relations expertise in devising their strategy. Kirk, a researcher in neuropsychiatry, and Madsen, a public relations consultant, argued that homosexuals must change their presentation to the heterosexual community if real success was to be made. They understood how to change completely a culture's view of the gay issue within a generation, although few believed it to be possible at the time. 'First you get your foot in the door,' they write:

> By being as similar as possible; then, and only then— when your one little difference is finally accepted—can you start dragging in your other peculiarities, one by one. You hammer in the wedge narrow end first. As the saying goes, 'Allow the camel's nose beneath your tent and his whole body will soon follow.'

Three ploys are to be taken up, they argue.

1. Desensitisation: 'To desensitize straights, Homosexuals inundate them with a conscious flood of Homosexual related advertising, presented in the least offensive fashion. If straights can't shut the shower off, they may at least eventually get used to being wet.'

2. Jamming: Jamming is more active and aggressive than desensitization, aiming to produce 'emotional dissonance' whereby people will for a while still have their previous feelings of revulsion but which are brought into conflict with new feelings of sympathy if not empathy. Propaganda is to be used whereby those who are traditional in their stance on the gay issue are portrayed as loud mouthed homophobes— rednecks of a Ku Klux Klan stripe (and no one wants to be associated with them, thus creating a feeling of shame), and such people should be shown to be disapproved of which in turn will 'cause them to keep

their heads down and mouths shut.' That is exactly what is happening.

3. Conversion: This is the ultimate goal. Kirk and Madsen say that if desensitization lets the watch run down, and jamming throws sand in the works, conversion reverses the spring so that the hands run backward:

Conversion of the average American's emotions, mind, and will, through a planned psychological attack, in the form of propaganda fed to the nation via the media. We mean 'subverting' the mechanism of prejudice to our own ends—using the very process that made America hate us, to turn their hatred into warm regard.

It is regarded as legitimate to use ads which lie to achieve this end:

It makes no difference that the ads are lies; not to us, because we're using them to ethically good effect, to counter negative stereotypes that are every bit as much lies, and far more wicked ones; not be bigots, because the ads will have their effect on them whether they believe them or not.

Goebbels would be proud

Propaganda is seen as key to achieving this. The authors point out three characteristics which distinguish propaganda from other modes of communication which contribute to its sinister reputation.

1. Relies on emotional manipulation—through desensitization, jamming and conversion

2. Uses lies

3. Is subjective and one-sided

This, however, is deemed necessary to 'win the peace campaign,' by telling the gay side of the story as movingly as possible. 'In the battle for hearts and minds, effective propaganda knows enough to put its best foot forward. This is what our own media campaign must do.' And they have done it so masterfully!

The gloves are off with regards to the church, which is seen as one of the main bastions of resistance to the gay movement. What is to be done? 'Gays can use talk to muddy the moral waters, that is, to undercut the rationalisations that "justify" religious bigotry and to jam some of its psychic rewards.' And to 'portray such institutions as antiquated backwaters, badly out of step with the times and with the latest findings of psychology.'

As Mohler observes:

A quick review of the last 15 years demonstrates the incredible effectiveness of this public relations advice. The agenda set out by Kirk and Madsen led to nothing less than social transformation. By portraying themselves as mainstream Americans seeking nothing but liberty and self-fulfilment, homosexuals redefined the moral equation. Issues of right and wrong were isolated as outdated, repressive, and culturally embarrassing. Instead, the assertion of 'rights' became the hallmark of the public relations strategy ... The advice offered by Marshall Kirk and Hunter Madsen is nothing less than a manifesto for moral revolution. A look back at this strategy indicates just how self-consciously the homosexual movement advanced its cause by following this plan.

The Persuaders

A number of years ago Os Guinness commented:

> Christians are always more culturally short-sighted than they realise. They are often unable to tell, for instance, where their Christian principles leave off and their cultural perspectives begin. What many of them fail to ask themselves is, 'where are we coming from and what is our own context?'

Christians are naïve to think they are not being influenced by marketing techniques

That is certainly the case when we consider the cultural shaping that has been taking place by the gay movement. If Christians think they are not being influenced by the kind of marketing techniques which the gay lobby is called to use by Kirk and Madsen, they simply need to watch the PBS 'Frontline' documentary *The Persuaders*. Kathryn C.Montgomery, former Professor of Communications at the University of California, writes:

> Although a number of lobby groups have campaigned

for exposure on the airwaves, the gay lobby has been by far the most organized and best coordinated, soon gaining a reputation as 'the most sophisticated and successful advocacy group operating in network television.'

All the main cultural transformers have been brought to bear to achieve this revolution. In addition to advertising, two other main vehicles of persuasion have been harnessed—the media and education.

Media magic

One of the most successful TV series in recent years is *Sex in the City*, a programme about a group of chic single women, who, as the title suggests, engage in a fairly free and easy sexual lifestyle. More recently, the idea of cheating on your partner and not telling them about it has been taken up by another TV series, *Desperate Housewives*. Infidelity has become the order of the day in much mainstream entertainment. Lee Siegel has argued that it is not coincidental that the creators of both *Sex in the City* and *Desperate Housewives* are all gay men. He suggests that what was going on was, 'an ingenious affirmation of a certain type of gay-male sexuality' which is notoriously promiscuous. This was brought to the fore by a ground-breaking survey in *The New York Times* in 2010 which revealed that about half of gay couples in San Francisco who were in a permanent relationship held to sexual openness, which, far from harming gay unions, is said to enrich them. Referring to *Sex in the City*, Siegel called it, 'the biggest hoax perpetrated on straight single women in the history of entertainment.' Single women who see themselves portrayed in these relationships are actually watching a justification for the gay men who produce the show. Therefore the portrayal of women behaving this way makes it easier to accept promiscuous homosexuality. In other words fiction is being used to perpetrate a fiction.

In 1996, the gay writer David Ehrenstein wrote an article in which he acknowledged '[t]here are openly gay writers on almost every major prime-time situation comedy you can think of.' He lists: *Friends*, *Seinfeld*, *Murphy Brown*, *Roseanne*, *Mad About You*, *The Nanny*, *Wings*, *The Single Guy*, *Caroline in the City*, *Coach*, *Dave's World*, *Home Court*, *High Society*, *The Crew* and *Boston Common*. Ehrenstein concludes: 'In short, when it comes to sitcoms, gays rule.'

Education, education, indoctrination

As the members of N.I.C.E. and the Frankfurt School recognised, capturing people's minds (and hearts) through education is central to any strategy for a lasting social revolution. As lesbian activist Patricia Warren notes, 'Whoever captures the kids, owns the future.'

This lies behind the Educate and Celebrate movement in the United Kingdom (which draws some of its funds from the BBC's Children in Need appeal). The web site reads:

> Educate & Celebrate is an Ofsted and DFE recognized Best Practice Award Programme that gives staff, students, parents and governors the confidence and strategies to

implement an LGBT+Inclusive curriculum to successfully eradicate homophobia, biphobia and transphobia from our nursery, primary and secondary schools, colleges, Universities, organisations and communities ... Our aim is to ensure that educational establishments and organisations adhere to their statutory duty of LGBT+Inclusion in an accessible, comprehensive and creative way by treating everyone equally and fairly according to the Equality Act 2010 ... Our own surveys in 2015 revealed that almost half our students across the country are not receiving any form of LGBT+Inclusive education with 53% of schools not teaching about LGBT+ relationships and 49% of schools not teaching the definitions of lesbian, gay, bisexual and trans+. In fact only 3% of schools said they had LGBT+ activity in 2 or more subject areas, which could explain why 76% of teachers said they'd had no LGBT+ specific training and 44% of schools contacted us initially because staff were not confident in dealing with sexual orientation or gender identity ... Educate & Celebrate responds to these needs by engaging all stakeholders in the journey to inclusion to make our educational establishments, organisations and communities LGBT+Friendly.

Warwickshire County Council have a web site called *Respect Yourself* designed to give advice on sexual relationships for young teenagers, containing this 'value free' assessment: 'Unfortunately, sex doesn't come with an instruction manual or map of the pitfalls and it certainly doesn't come with a moral compass. People see sex in many different lights and have sex for many different reasons.' Little wonder that teenage pregnancies continue to rise along with anxiety amongst the young.

Parson Street Primary School in Bristol invited Drag Queen Story Time to read books promoting alternative lifestyles to their children. Drag Queen Story Time founder Tom Canham said:

> We have an opportunity to provide our children with a better world in which to grow up, free from fear of rejection, or abuse, for being who they are—and Drag Queen Story Time is proud to be working with fantastic organisations all across the country to help make that a reality.

Silencing the lambs

We have already noted Marcuse's uncompromising attitude to dissidents, that certain ideas are not to be expressed (and it is a short step from forbidding the expression of ideas to banning ideas). This is now working itself out aggressively in our various institutions.

In 2016 Felix Ngole had said during a Facebook debate that 'the Bible and God identify homosexuality as a sin.' On the basis of this he was removed from his two year MA course in Social Work at the University of Sheffield. Writing in *The Sun* columnist Rod Liddle commented:

> Frankly, I think our social services departments could do with rather more people who have strong, Christian principles instead of the inept, hand-wringing, liberal halfwits allowed the vile abuse of children to go on

across the country ... But even that's not the main point. Universities are supposed to be places where a huge diversity of views can be heard. Not any more, not in our universities. If you don't subscribe to every one of their modern, secular, liberal beliefs you're out on your ear. Either banned from speaking at their campuses or thrown off your course. Just because you believe in something that they don't.

Marcuse would no doubt rub his hands in glee over the UK universities, over which the 'hideous strength' casts its long dark shadow.

Get connected

We have spoken of Babel-connectivity and N.I.C.E. using technology; both of these come together today with today's social media. Whole causes can be orchestrated becoming worldwide news (fake or otherwise) within a matter of hours. Furthermore, Marcuse's call to silence those who would oppose the revolution has become much easier with a lynch mob mentality being able to be whipped up with ease via Facebook, Twitter and the like. Understandably with such a possibility of this happening people will want to keep their heads down and mouths shut!

'This new "sexual" agenda is ... a remaking of human "identity",' writes Professor Peter Jones:

We are dealing with a neo-Marxism so committed to a classless egalitarian society that it must eradicate by any means possible embodied gender distinctions, which are the final bulwark of creational difference, written into our DNA. The goal is no longer a classless society but a classless mind and a genderless body—no longer just a fair deal for the worker but a transformation of the human psyche! At this point, such a powerful cosmology takes on an unmistakably religious character.

There are two institutions which are seen to be barriers to achieving this agenda and both are intrinsically related: the family and the church, to which we now turn.

Chapter 5
Barbarians through the gates

WHILE APPEARING TO PORTRAY GAY MARRIAGE AND GAY families as simply variants along a sociological spectrum, the end game of the neo-Marxist agenda is the destruction of the family.

Unhappy families

I have already considered the influence of Marcuse and the promotion of polymorphous perversity, but this required the abolition of the traditional patriarchal family:

> No longer used as a full-time instrument of labour, the body would be resexualized, (which) would first manifest itself in a reactivation of all erotogenic zones and, consequently, in a resurgence of pregenital polymorphous sexuality and in a decline of genital supremacy. The body in its entirety would become an object of cathexis, a thing to be enjoyed—an instrument of pleasure. This change in the value and scope of libidinal relations would lead to

a disintegration of the institutions in which the private interpersonal relations have been reorganized, particularly the monogamic and patriarchal family.

The intention is clear—destroy the family.

Others have been more explicit in their aim. For example, the Gay Liberation Front Manifesto states:

> Equality is never going to be enough; what is needed is a total social revolution, a complete reordering of civilization. Reform ... cannot change the deep-down attitude of straight people that homosexuality is at best inferior to their own way of life, at worst a sickening perversion. It will take more than reforms to change this attitude, because it is rooted in our society's most basic institution—the Patriarchal Family.

More recently, the Lesbian author and activist Masha Gessen let the proverbial gay cat out of the neo-Marxist bag when she said:

> Fighting for gay marriage generally involves lying about what we're going to do with marriage when we get there. Because we lie that the institution of marriage is not going to change, and that is a lie. The institution of marriage is going to change and it should change, and again, I don't think it should exist.

It is therefore somewhat disturbing to find the Archbishop of Canterbury, Justin Welby, acquiescing to this redefinition and slow destruction of the family. In a lecture he delivered in Moscow in 2017, Welby said:

The place where most people forge their first relationships is within the family. It is easy, however, *to define what makes up the family very narrowly* ... The reality is that family life is and always has been complex. In the United Kingdom in the last forty years there has been a great shift in the understanding and the reality of family life ... In recent years in a number of nations, including the United Kingdom, same-sex, or as it is called in law, equal marriage is now understood to be normal, acceptable and unchallengeable in many countries ... The speed of change has led many constituencies such as churches and other faith groups to find themselves living in a culture that they have not even begun to come to terms with ... The family, *however it is experienced*, is the place where we can be at our strongest and most secure ... It is a gift of God in any society, bearing burdens, supporting the vulnerable and stabilising both those who believe themselves autonomous and those who feel themselves to be failures (emphasis mine).

> *Welby unthinkingly falls into the neo-Marxist line by calling the family a malleable concept*

It is obvious that the Archbishop wants to defend and strengthen the place of the family in society, but by implying that biblical norms regarding what constitutes family are too 'narrowly defined,' Welby unthinkingly falls into line with the neo-Marxist drum beat that the family is a malleable concept which can (and should) be changed or even got rid of altogether. More recently in his book, *Reimagining Britain*, Welby is even more positive about same-sex marriage when he writes:

> Same-sex marriage builds on the presumption that marriage is stable and lifelong (the rootedness of the tradition), while also responding to the massive shift in cultural acceptance with regard to the understanding of human nature and sexual orientation.

One may well think with friends like these who needs enemies?

Will Jones, may be scathing in his criticism of the Archbishop but his logic is flawless when he writes:

> If this is in fact the case, then from a traditional Christian point of view it is baffling, not to mention seriously endangering Christian moral living and integrity of witness to the revelation of God in Christ. For in what other area of life, other than this one of sex, gender and family, would it be thought appropriate to encourage the church merely to come to terms with contemporary realities, and not to evaluate them, challenge them, and point to a better way in closer conformity with the Creator's designs? There are many complex realities, alongside broken families and wounded childhoods, with which modern people live—drug addiction, alcohol abuse, the sexualisation of children, corruption, destitution, slavery—yet for how many of them would the church counsel, or even appear to counsel, Christians merely to accept them and come to terms with them with no further comment or analysis?

The apparent surrender of the church to the world's ideas in this particular area of sex, marriage and family is deeply disturbing to observe—not unlike watching a car crash in slow motion.

Traditionally the church has been the bastion of the family and so capturing the church is strategic if the revolution is to be completed and the 'hideous strength' is to hold sway. More so, if one of the more traditional denominations cracks, that will have a far greater impact on public perception.

Burning down the house

The two church institutions which are primary targets for the sex revisionist agenda are the Roman Catholic Church and the Church of England.

The Roman Catholic Church has been perceived by the public at least, to be traditional in its position on heterosexual marriage and the unacceptability of same-sex relations. That seems to be changing under Pope Francis. In 2015 he appointed Dominican Father Timothy Radcliffe as a consultor for the Pontifical Council for Justice and Peace. As a contributor to the 2013 Church of England Pilling Report on human sexual ethics, Father Radcliffe said of homosexuality:

How does all of this bear on the question of gay sexuality? We cannot begin with the question of whether it is permitted or forbidden! We must ask what it means, and how far it is Eucharistic. Certainly it can be generous, vulnerable, tender, mutual and non-violent. So in many ways, I would think that it can be expressive of Christ's self-gift. We can also see how it can be expressive of mutual fidelity, a covenantal relationship in which two people bind themselves to each other for ever.

We saw in the character of the Revd Straik in Lewis's novel how religious terminology was skilfully used as a Trojan horse to promote naturalistic materialism, something similar is now happening in the promotion of a new paganism.

Similarly religious language is used and abused to make the Bible say the opposite of what it does say, thus scaling heaven to bring God down.

Old heresies in new guises

In July 2017, Jayne Ozanne (who claims to be evangelical) placed a private member's motion to the General Synod meeting in York calling upon the Synod to effectively repudiate the practice of conversion therapy for those who experience same-sex attraction. Contained in her summary statement is a heresy which no one thought to challenge:

The Bible teaches us that we are each fearfully and wonderfully made (Psalm 139:14), and that we should praise God's gift of our creation. Thus, our diversity as human beings is a reflection of God's creativity and something to celebrate. The biblical concern is not with what we are but how we choose to live our lives, meaning that differing sexual orientations and gender identities are not inherently sinful, nor mental health disorders to be 'cured.'

The partial truth, which is being taken and exaggerated as the whole truth, appears in the first sentence of her quotation. This has been taken by Christians in the past as a basis for the sanctity of human life which is undermined by the practice of abortion. However, it is a *non sequitur* for Ozanne to then conclude 'Thus, our diversity as human beings is a reflection of God's creativity and something to celebrate.' If anything, as we have noted, it is the belief in human sanctity which is to be protected which logically arises out of this passage, not human diversity. This is followed up by falsehood for it is certainly not the case that the Bible isn't concerned with 'what we are' but simply 'how we choose to live our lives.' How we choose and what we choose at least in part arises from 'what we are.' Some of those dispositions are towards things which God forbids (such as idolatry, greed and same-sex relations) and not only flow from 'what we are' (idolaters, gluttons, homosexuals, etc.) but reinforces what we are becoming.

> *The missing doctrine which is necessary to check is the doctrine of original sin*

The missing doctrine which is necessary to check the heresy Ozanne and her supporters like the Bishop of Liverpool, Paul Bayes, are promoting is the doctrine of original sin. To be sure, according to the psalmist we are 'fearfully and wonderfully made,' but according to the same psalmist in Psalm 51:5, 'I was sinful at birth, sinful from the time my mother conceived me.' At both one and the same time, David is 'fearfully and wonderfully made' in the womb and 'sinful' from the moment he was conceived. We are, as Immanuel Kant once said, 'warped wood,' or, again, as Luther put it, '*incurvartus in se*,' or even, to use traditional terminology, contaminated by original sin which, according to Article 9 of the 39 articles of the Church of England, is 'the fault and corruption of Nature of everyman ... and is of his own nature inclined to evil.'

Jayne Ozanne is effectively promoting two heresies at once.

The first is Pelagianism.

In the fifth century, the monk Pelagius argued that 'Evil is not born with us, and we are procreated without fault; and the only thing in men at their birth is what God has formed.' This was effectively dealt with by St Augustine and condemned decisively at the Council of Carthage in 418 with the condemnation being ratified at the Council of Ephesus in 431.

The second heresy, called Socinianism, is a variation of the first and is named after its exponent, Faustus Socinus. This teaching has been effectively summarized by Andrew Fuller:

> They consider all evil propensities in men (except those which are accidently contracted by education or example) as

being, in every sense, natural to them; supposing that they were originally created with them; they cannot, therefore be offensive to God, unless he could be offended with the work of his own hands for being what he made it.

But this is to engage with issues in terms of reason and argument which is shunned by cultural Marxism as being tactically dangerous. Far better to throw in a few positive phrases such as being 'fearfully and wonderfully made' so that those who are seen to be questioning the proponent appear to be the heretical ones!

The way in which cultural Marxism has triumphed in the General Synod of the Church of England as reflected in the Ozanne debate (even if it has not been recognised as such) has been well articulated by the General Synod member, Dr Chik Kaw Tan. He observes that at Synod, 'Theology is seen to get in the way of real life. The little theological context there is focuses on love, acceptance, equality and justice,' the very stuff of Marcuse. He further reflects:

12 years ago when I first joined Synod, the LGBT lobby consisted of a little stand with a few people handing out leaflets. Many Synod members subtly changed the direction of movement away from them and politely avoided any conversation with LGBT activists. 12 years on, they are the all-winning victorious juggernaut, crushing all in its path. Not only is the LGBT constituency well and truly embedded in the organisational structure of the Church of England, its agenda for change dominates proceedings.

The LGBT long march has almost arrived at its final destination in the Church of England.

No sanctity in sex please—we're religious

Sometimes non-Christians on the outside seem to be more insightful about the church than Christians who are on the inside.

Camille Paglia is one such person.

In her essay, 'The Joy of Presbyterian Sex' she exposes the neo-Marxist gullibility of much liberal Christianity. Writing about the Presbyterian Church's report on Human sexuality (USA), she comments,

> The committee's prescription for an enlightened Christianity is 'learning from the marginalized.' This new liberal cliché is repeated so often that I began to misread it as 'margarinized.' We are told that 'those of us with varying degrees of social power and status must now move away from the center, so that other, more marginalized voices ... may be heard.' But the report picks and chooses its marginalized outcasts as snobbishly as Proust's Duchesse de Guermantes. We can move tender, safe, clean, hand-holding gays and lesbians to the center—but not, of course, pederasts, prostitutes, strippers, pornographers, or sadomasochists. And if we're going to learn from the marginalized, what about drug dealers, moonshiners, Elvis impersonators, string collectors, Mafiosi foot fetishists, serial murderers, cannibals, Satanists, and the Ku Klux Klan? I'm sure they'll all have a lot to say. The committee

gets real prudish real fast when it has to deal with sexuality outside its feminist frame of reference: 'Incest is abhorrent and abhorred,' it flatly declares. I wrote in the margin, 'No lobbyists, I guess!'

Carl Trueman in pondering Paglia's remarks asks, 'So why do Christians capitulate to such nonsense so easily?' He answers:

> Here Paglia and I are on the same page: Because the Christian church is too often not satisfied with being the Christian church, with all of its austere dogma and demands, but prefers to be merely an insipid and derivative mouthpiece for modern emotivism. Liberal churches do what they always do: In an effort to remain credible they dutifully turn up to baptize whatever sentimental mush the world wants to promote on the trendy topic of the moment. Of course, it always does this a day or two late, but that's what happens when your ethics are simply a response to norms which the world has already embraced. No longer is it 'Thus saith the Lord!' so much as 'Now, now, poor dear, you just do what feels right for you. Oh, and please, whatever you do, don't feel guilty about it.'

The church increasingly adds its own confused voice to the confusing voices of the culture

The church increasingly adds its own confused voice to the confusing voices of the Babel culture in which it finds itself. Marcuse's goal to 'destabilise language' is being helped along by the double speak of the church.

Blurring the boundaries

The exchange of a biblical cosmology for a new pagan one is also much in evidence in the Church of England as shown by the recent debates on gender.

Following the affirmation of transgender people in the July 2017 General Synod and the House of Bishops permission to clergy to adapt liturgy to indicate acknowledgement of gender change, the trajectory is clear as are the underlying views regarding sexuality. It is now expected that churches simply accept that a transgender person is not just identifying a gender different from his/her biological sex, but that he/she is ontologically different. This is a new narrative. No longer is a transgender person someone who feels trapped in the wrong body, this is a new variant of what it means to be human. The boundaries of creation have not simply been set aside, they have been wiped away.

This is fully in-line with the liberation desired by the cultural Marxists; if sexual identity is a social construct like everything else, then use technology to bring nature into line. But this is completely contrary to the biblical vision which is ably described by Professor Oliver O'Donovan:

> One can express the Christian perspective like this: the either-or of biological maleness and femaleness to which

the human race is bound is not a meaningless or oppressive condition of nature; it is the good gift of God, because it gives rise to possibilities of relationship in which the polarities of masculine and feminine, more subtly nuanced than the biological differentiation, can play a decisive part.

Culture clash

Here the clash of cosmologies signified by the Tower of Babel is brought into sharp focus. Either there is objective reality to which we are to conform our minds, senses and values and so have genuine human flourishing within the boundaries God has given, or all such claims are to be regarded with suspicion and further expressions of repressive tolerance. Os Guinness remarks:

When God removes the boundaries in judgment, creation collapses in on itself in chaos

The story of creation is a story of distinctions, a story of discrimination between heaven and earth, which the Tower of Babel tries to undo, between male and female, etc. In fact, the Jews called the Lord, 'the Great Discriminator,' because His creation discriminates between things, and if you remove the discriminations, you create idols; they're much closer in their understanding of the deadliness of some of the ideas at the heart of the sexual revolution.

When God removes the boundaries in judgment,

creation collapses in on itself in chaos as at the Flood; when we begin to remove the boundaries, society collapses in on itself in excessive self-confidence.

Although it is a distasteful subject the next blurring of the boundaries is not between human sexes, but human and non-human—zoophilia. Here we see the full corruption of human hubris. Journalist, Malcolm J. Brenner, achieved notoriety by having sex with a dolphin; the subject of his award winning documentary *Dolphin Lover*. He describes himself as a zoophile. He believes his zoophilia is the result of the 'very intense physical and sexual abuse' he claims to have suffered in early childhood at the hands of psychologist Albert Duvall, a student of the controversial psychoanalyst Wilhelm Reich of the Frankfurt School. 'I think I found animals to be a safe and secure repository for my sexual desires,' he says in the documentary. Brenner draws parallels between current anti-bestiality laws and the anti-miscegenation laws of the nineteenth and twentieth centuries in the USA because, as he says in the documentary, '150 years ago, black people were considered a degenerate sub-species of the human being … And I'm hoping that in a more enlightened future, zoophilia will be no more regarded as controversial or harmful than interracial sex is today.'

Others, like Cody Beck, draw a different parallel; being a zoophile in modern American society, Beck says, is 'like being gay in the 1950s. You feel like you have to hide, that if you say it out loud, people will look at you like a freak.' It is difficult to argue against this if the neo-Marxist thesis is correct regarding social constructionism. But people do argue against it on moral grounds. For example, Piers Beirne, author of *Confronting Animal Abuse,* says that because there is an imbalance of power involved, the animals which are sexually engaged in this way are invariably domestic 'completely dependent upon us for food, water, shelter and affection.' He concludes, 'I think it is morally wrong for a human to have sex with non-human animals for exactly the same reason it's wrong for him to have sex with human babies or adolescents.' But what is the moral basis for arguing that it is the imbalance of power which is the morally deciding factor? Why should this be regarded as morally wrong? If one were to adopt a consequentialist approach to ethics, that such activity could be shown to be harmful to those involved and wider society in the long run, then that might have some traction. But of course if one were to go down this line then one would have to apply the same reasoning to homosexual behaviour and promiscuity, which people are loathed to do. We are back to a neo-Marxist concern that abuse of power is the only thing that is forbidden.

The abolition of God and the abolition of man

The end result of all neo-Marxist philosophies is not the liberation of human beings but their destruction—'the abolition of man.' Let us not be under any illusions as to what is at stake. Hannah Arendt showed in her reporting of the trial of Hitler's chief architect of the Final Solution, Adolf Eichmann, that he and those like him were only able to carry out their atrocities by separating themselves from their victims by denying the common humanity which connected them both. In the words of Carl Trueman in his essay 'The Banality of Evil', 'The possibility of the Final Solution was predicated on the abolition of common human nature.' If there is no common human nature, it is difficult to see what basis there is for human rights. Why should this too be any less of a social construct, one which can be made and unmade by the dominant social class of the time? Indeed, for the cultural Marxist such rights need to be formulated and given legislative force to impose the new liberty. If it is a human right for those who are gay to marry, it will be unacceptable to have a society which refuses it. It will be forbidden to forbid.

Hopefully by now it is clear that, as was the case with the Studdocks in Lewis's novel, countless 'pitiful souls' in the West, many of them children, have become the 'apocalyptic battleground of heaven.'

How should the church respond?

Chapter 6
Bringing Down Babel

THE PICTURE WHICH HAS BEEN PAINTED SEEMS RATHER bleak. But the church has had to face similar situations before. The Babel story repeats itself again and again throughout world history that, in the words of G.K. Chesterton, 'At least five times ... the Faith has to all appearances gone to the dogs. In each of these five cases, it was the dog that died.'

> *The picture may seem bleak, but the church has faced similar situations*

In the aftermath of ruins of the Second World War, theologian Emile Brunner wrote:

Sometimes I even think it is already too late. At any rate, if by the mercy of God we are to have some further breathing space, if He does grant us another chance to build up a new European civilization on the ruins of the old, facing all the time the possibility of an imminent end to all civilized life on this globe, Christianity has a tremendous responsibility.

That responsibility has not diminished in the twenty-first century.

Our hope as Christian believers against the 'hideous strength' is to be found within the account of the Tower of Babel itself.

Let me explain.

The story is presented in a chiastic structure which depicts a reversal of humankind's plans with the centre point being Genesis 11:5:

A 'the whole world had one language' (v. 1)
    B 'there' (v. 2)
        C 'each other' (v. 3)
            D 'Come, let's make bricks' (v. 3)
                E 'Come, let us build ourselves' (v. 4)
                    F 'a city, with a tower' (v. 4)
                        G *the LORD came down* (v. 5)
                    F^I 'the city and the tower' (v. 5)
                E^I 'that men were building' (v. 5)
            D^I 'Come, let us … confuse' (v. 7)
        C^I 'each other' (v. 7)
    B^I 'from there' (v. 8)
A^I 'the language of the whole world' (v. 9)

Not only is the 'reversal' construction clearly visible, but it also paints a picture. When this diagram is turned on its

side, the narrative of the Tower of Babel forms a picture of
the Tower of Babel:

> YHWH's deliberation
> YHWH comes down–let us come down
> tower's top in heaven–on surface of the earth
> name for ourselves————name called Babel
> lest we be scattered ————YHWH scattered them
> let us build a city ————they stopped building the city
> settlement in Shinar ————-YHWH scattered them
> one language for all ————-YHWH confuses their languages
> all the earth————over the face of all the earth

In both representations it is *Yahweh's* action, not
humankind's, which is final and decisive. Despite
humankind's attempt to redefine and reconfigure reality—
to 'de-god God'—it is God in his glorious omnipotence
and infinite wisdom who remains Lord. He subverts all
our attempts to subvert, and his great reality, which lies
behind all realities, will win out.

While people use various means and idolatries to try and
'bring God down,' it is God who elects to come down and
take captive all the rulers and
authorities and principalities
and powers. What verse 5
embodies is a principle which
lies at the heart of the Bible,
that *God comes down in both
judgment and mercy.* This was
the basis for the hope of the

God subverts our attempts to subvert, his great reality will win out

Hebrew slaves in Exodus 3:8, 'I have come down.' Scott
Oliphint comments:

> These four words could easily serve to frame the core of
> our understanding of God from Genesis to Revelation.
> There is no way to understand both who God is and his
> dealings with his creation without seeing it through this
> principle running throughout Scripture.

It is this principle which finds its climax in the
incarnation of the Eternal Logos, whose light still shines
and is not mastered by darkness (John 1:5).

Christians have to carefully navigate between the Scylla
of dewy-eyed optimism and the Charybdis of faithless
pessimism. On the one hand the hold of modernity on the
church can foster a can-do mentality which mimics that of
the builders of the Tower of Babel—where employing the
latest marketing techniques and following church growth
indicators produces mega churches (although they may
be little more than Christianised versions of the culture to
which they are held captive). On the other hand, a high
sounding pietism marks a cultural retreat as, secure in
their own subculture, evangelicals, in particular, remain
doctrinally sound but become culturally irrelevant and
their voice is not heard. Os Guinness strikes the right
biblical note which lies at the centre of the Babel episode
emphasising *God's* action:

> Let it be clearly understood that our hope in the
> possibility of renewal is squarely grounded, not in ourselves,
> not in history and the fact that it has happened before,

but in the power of God demonstrated by the truth of the resurrection of Jesus ... This is therefore no time to hang our heads or hide our lights under any bushel for fear that we may be picked on for our refusal to fit in. We are to have no fear. We are to look up. We are to take strength from the fact that we can, because he can.

Get real

Three things are necessary if, like Ransom and his small band of believers in Lewis's story, we are to challenge the 'hideous strength' in its present cultural Marxist form, namely, commending God's Truth, cultural engagement and courageous refusal and refutation.

Commending God's truth

If metaphysics is the study of 'what is', theology is the presentation of 'what is in Christ'. The church of Christ should be in the business of presenting reality which comes from 'above' rather than trying to attempt with the world to reconstruct reality from 'below' with Babel hubris.

Three things are to be to at the fore of the church's reality check.

> *The church must hold out the reality of Christ*

First, the church must hold on to and hold out the reality of God in Christ, that is, his true *deity*—'the Word made flesh.' This is not a malleable God we can make in our own image. One that conforms to our idolatrous ideas and desires, or one that is domesticated and brought down according to our whim. He is the Creator who by a word stills the storm (Mark 4:35–41) and stops the forces of chaos (Mark 5:1–20). He comes to us as Judge who will not tolerate the established religious leaders who, by their man made traditions, nullify the Word of God (Mark 7:1–23), and who cause little ones to stumble (Mark 9:42–50). He comes as Saviour to do that which we cannot do, reconcile us to God by his atoning sacrifice on the cross (Mark 10:45). As Vanhoozer writes in *The Pastor as Public Theologian*, 'Everything Jesus says, does and is reveals God. What there is in Christ is true knowledge of God.'

In the second place what is in Christ is true *humanity*. This man Jesus (yes, biologically male with X and Y chromosomes having a real human nature, which he still has in heaven seated at God's right hand) is the Son of Man, the Second Adam, showing us what it means to live the other-person centred life in complete delightful obedience to his Father. The model of Christ runs counter to the cultural Marxism in which human nature disappears together with human rights. Human nature, which the Second person of the Trinity assumed, is divinely given, not humanly fabricated. The undermining of the one will invariably lead to an undermining of the other.

The battle for the Christ

It is not insignificant that the main battles in the early church against heresy centred on the blurring of the boundaries with regards to the person and nature of Jesus of Nazareth. There was the heresy of Arianism in the fourth century which denied the *deity* of Christ, viewing him as some kind of 'super-creature' who was *like* God the Father (Greek: *homoiousios*), but not of the same substance as the Father (Greek: *homoousios*). This was roundly condemned by the Council of Nicaea in 325.

Gnosticism on the other hand, denied the *humanity* of Christ; he only seemed to be human. Eutychianism in the fifth century postulated Christ as a 'hybrid,' a chimera of deity and humanity, neither fully human nor fully divine but a third type of being, a man/god. The church, however, wished to do full justice to the boundaries God had established in this unique self-revelation, as formulated in Chalcedon in 451, that Jesus Christ was in nature fully man, fully divine, not confused or mixed, but two natures in one person. All heresies try to bring God down in true Babel fashion, but God chooses to come down in the way he has established.

We should not be surprised that the present gender confusion leads to a confusion on the person and nature of Christ

We should not therefore be surprised that as there is a

confusing of boundaries in the present gender debates within the church today, there is also a confusing of the person and nature of Christ. Such distinctions as 'divinity,' 'humanity' and 'sonship' suggest hierarchy and difference which the neo-Marxist cannot tolerate. And so we have this in a creed from the early 1990s declared at a World Council of Churches conference, 'I believe in God, MOTHER-FATHER-SPIRIT who called the world into being, who created men and women and set them free to live in love, in obedience and community.' The publisher, LBI Institute, released a Bible entitled: *Judith Christ of Nazareth, The Gospels of the Bible, Corrected to Reflect that Christ Was a Woman,* Extracted *from Matthew, Mark, Luke and John.* These are further examples of 'breaking the established universe of meaning' central to the cultural Marxist strategy.

Third, what is in Christ is the whole created order, made by him sustained by him, having its goal in him, 'All things were created through him and for him ... and in him all things hold together' (Colossians 1:16–17). It is an order and created thus having a design and purpose; boundaries and spaces, which is determined by the Creator, not the creatures. In the Lord Jesus Christ, creation has a telos, a goal and end point, and so contrary to the assertions of the postmodernists, there is an overarching story, a metanarrative. As Vanhoozer writes in 'Sapientail Apologetics', 'To think theologically is to understand persons, events and things (the parts) in relation to what is in Christ (the whole).'

These are some of the central immutable 'non-negotiables' of the faith 'delivered once and for all to the saints' and the task of the church is to think and act theologically in understanding God, the world and ourselves in relation to Christ. However, getting to grips with theology is only one half of the task, the other half is to understand our culture in order to be effective agents of change for Christ in the culture.

Cultural engagement

The church is easily drawn towards one of two extremes.

At one pole is what Peter Berger calls *cognitive and cultural resistance*. Here the biblical call to flee the idols of the world in 1 Thessalonians 1:9 leads to a cultural isolation from the world as Christians form their own sub-culture which may owe more to fear than faithfulness. Such churches keep the world at a distance while making the occasional foray in evangelism. But they always remain feeling safe and secure with their preaching, fearing to say anything that might upset the powers that be, either in government or the church, for fear of having those privileges taken away (while of course not realizing that such privileges are being eroded while they remain silent).

Parallels have been drawn with the situation of the church in pre-war Nazi Germany. In her article 'While The Church Sleeps ...' Lisa Nolland makes the astute observation that:

> We look back on the 1930s with angry incredulity at the

blindness of German Christian leaders. How could they have ignored events at the heart of public life, occurring before their very eyes? Well, are we any different? The press of preaching duties, conferences, programmes, financial and pastoral crises, etc., mean that politically-incorrect, controversial issues just get buried. The herd/tribe mentality is as strong as that of 'Let's just be positive. God is good, all the time!' The culture in church circles is a million miles away from that of many secular workplaces. Moreover there are potent but subconscious assumptions made by leaders. Given (almost daily) LGBT conditioning, many in their flock now 'see the light', but because of the subconscious but tacit 'don't ask, don't tell', aren't saying.

At the other extreme is *cognitive and cultural adaptation* which is the seduction of the church by culture. This is a four stage process.

1. *Assumption*: when some idea in modern life is assumed to be worthwhile and superior to Christian belief.

2. *Abandonment*: so whatever in the Christian faith doesn't fit in with the new assumption is either modified or jettisoned.

3. *Adaptation*: something new is assumed, something old is abandoned, everything else is adapted so that while what the church is espousing still has some semblance of genuine Christianity, it is significantly modified.

4. *Assimilation*: what is left is absorbed by the modern

world and effectively taken over. What passes for Christianity is simply reflecting back to the world its own values and ideas in a thinly veiled Christian dress. Christian words are used, but the Christian content is removed. This also is an instance of Marcuse's strategy to 'break the established universe of meaning.'

The Tower of Babel is being built, the secularists are the architects and some church leaders (including Bishops) and their advisors are the artisans. The problem which arises when the Church does this was bluntly put by Reinhold Niebuhr:

The modern church regards this mundane interest as its social passion. But it is also the mark of its slavery to society. Whenever religion feels completely at home in the world, it is the salt which has lost its savour. If it sacrifices the strategy of renouncing the world it has no strategy by which it may convict the world of sin.

Evangelicals are prone to think that they would never be tempted to go down this route. But as we have seen, the all-pervading nature of cultural Marxism and the subversive methods it employs can take evangelicals unawares as much as anyone else. Here is a pertinent observation by David Robertson of what has happened to some evangelicals in the Church of Scotland on the homosexuality debate:

Over ten years ago when the whole SSM and homosexuality debate began in the C of S [Church of

Scotland] I got in enormous trouble and 'hurt' people for
saying that the evangelicals were being suckered by the
Establishment. The response was that this was a battle that
they would win, that two evangelicals had been invited on
to the panel to investigate the matter that an evangelical was
going to become Moderator, etc. But they were suckered.
Big time. The evangelicals were never allowed to outnumber
the liberals. The only reason they were invited on to these
groups was to enable them to keep their fellow evangelicals
in line. They were invited to the table but they were not
allowed any say in the menu. They were outmanoeuvred
every time by fine words, appeals to unity (and to pride),
threats and empty promises of jam tomorrow. I have to
say that from a liberal perspective it was a brilliant strategy
that largely worked—mainly because the evangelicals
were leaderless, clueless and blinded by a myopic fixation
with what they hoped the Church of Scotland could be,
not what it really is—(as well as a genuine concern for
their own congregations). Most evangelicals stayed in, but
not to fight. Now they have been reassimilated into the
Establishment to such a degree that they are completely
toothless.

The same is now happening to evangelicals within the
Church of England.

There is, however, a third way exemplified by Paul in
1 Corinthians 9, namely, *cognitive and cultural negotiation*,
holding firm to the faith delivered once and for all to the
saints and being flexible in how this is expressed—'being

all things to all men in order to save some.' Paul's way brings us into cultural engagement with the Gospel.

Courageous refusal

With confidence in the reality that is in Christ (genuine theology), the church must eschew seductive approaches to accommodate to culture and instead embrace a more costly path.

> *With confidence in Christ, the church must eschew seductive approaches to accommodate culture*

It was C.S. Lewis who pointed out that the strength of the church's apologetic lay in going against the spirit of the age. In his essay, 'Christian Apologetics Today', written at the same time as *That Hideous Strength*, he outlines the basis for what he calls 'resistance thinking.' This is:

A way of thinking that balances the pursuit of relevance on the one hand with a tenacious awareness of those elements of the Christian message that don't fit in with any contemporary age on the other. Emphasize only the natural fit between the gospel and the spirit of the age and we will have an easy, comfortable gospel that is closer to our age than to the gospel—all answers to human aspirations, for example, and no mention of self-denial and sacrifice. But emphasize the difficult, the obscure, and even the repellent themes of the gospel, certain that they too are relevant even though we don't know how, and we will remain true to the full gospel. And, surprisingly, we will be relevant not only to our own generation but also the next, and the next and the next ... Resistance thinking, then, is the way of relevance with faithfulness.

Similarly, Harry Blamires writes:

Christians have always accepted that their spiritual and moral position vis-à-vis the unbelieving world does not in essentials change. Our reliance upon the Bible as the Word of God presupposes that advice given in one age is valid for another. The pattern of Christian preaching established over the centuries is based on the assumption that the Christian message is unalterable in its essentials.

Both the feasibility and desirability from a Biblical viewpoint of 'going against the flow' is borne out by various studies. A number of years ago Dean Kelley showed that by and large conservative churches grow and liberal churches decline because liberal churches offer commodities such as 'fellowship, entertainment and knowledge' which are also provided by secular institutions, while conservative churches offer 'the one incentive which is unique to churches': salvation, 'the promise of supernatural life after death.'

Stark and Finke have drawn attention to the self-destructive nature of theological liberalism in relation to the work of Don Cupitt:

Why should religion without God have a future? Cupitt's prescription strikes us as rather like expecting people who continue to buy soccer tickets and gather in the stands to watch players who, for lack of a ball, just stand around. If there are no supernatural beings, then there are no miracles, there is no salvation, prayer is pointless, the Commandments are but ancient wisdom, and death is the end. In which case, the rational person would have nothing to do with church. Or, more accurately, a rational person would have nothing to do with a church like that.

In his own inimitable way, G.K. Chesterton, writing in *The Everlasting Man*, pinpointed the issue, 'A dead thing can go with the stream, but only a living thing can go against it.' This doesn't mean that we should simply remain close to theological orthodoxy without being culturally engaged to cause growth—patently that is not the case—but it does underscore the importance of maintaining Christian distinctiveness in belief and behaviour as God's chosen people living, in the words of 1 Peter 1:1, as strangers (exiles) in the world.

The picture of Christians being in exile is suggestive of how we are to relate and witness in an increasingly hostile culture living in the shadow of the present Tower of Babel.

In *The Pastor as Public Theologian*, Vanhoozer calls one of the major New Testament themes 'joyful endurance.' This was the characteristic of the early church when it stood against the world to save it, rather than go along with the world and be lost with it. In Hebrews 10:32–33, the writer reminds his readers of the time they had been 'publically exposed [*theatrizo*] to abuse and affliction.' Within the theatre of faith the truth of the reality in Christ endures. Unlike the Tower of 'hideous strength' which eventually collapses under its own weight, Christ's building is one against which, Matthew 16:18 makes clear, 'the gates of hell will not prevail.'

Courageous refutation

This brings us to the second aspect of Christian courage, courageous refutation.

To speak of courageous refusal can appear to be a kind of active passivity, like the picture of a man hunched up against the wind, he refuses to be blown sideways and his activity is simply standing firm and not moving (the passive part). But those in the past who have made the greatest impact for the cause of truth have also been those who have engaged with the culture, exposing and refuting it and being willing to pay the price in terms of attracting the culture's reproach.

Those who have made the greatest impact for the truth have been those who have been willing to pay the price of cultural reproach

Without doubt, one of the greatest men God used in the late-eighteenth and early-nineteenth centuries to bring about a social, political and spiritual change in Great Britain was William Wilberforce. On Sunday 28 October 1787, Wilberforce wrote in his diary, 'God Almighty has set before me two great objects, the suppression of the Slave Trade and the Reformation of Manners,' by which he meant the reform of the morals of Britain. His tireless efforts to abolish the slave trade are well known, for which he paid a great price in terms of his reputation (Lord Nelson said that he should have been flogged, and scandalous rumours were spread that the reason he was so keen on freeing black slaves was because he himself kept a black mistress). His second great aim, however, is less well known, but serves as an example of a courageous refutation of the 'hideous strength' of his age.

For Wilberforce politics could only go so far, he wrote:

> I should be an example of that false shame which I have condemned in others were I not to admit boldly my firm conviction that our national difficulties must both directly and indirectly be ascribed to the decline of [Christian] religion and morality. The only solid hopes for the well-being of our country depend not so much on her fleets and armies, the wisdom of her rulers, or the spirit of her people, as on the realisation that she still contains many, who, in a degenerate age, love and obey the Gospel of Christ. My humble trust is that the prayers of these may still prevail and that, for their sake, God may still favour us.

He knew that anything else was cosmetic and short lived. What was needed was for men and women to be brought into restored relationship with their Maker through Jesus Christ and changed by his Spirit. He decided to pen an apologetic work, now under the title, *Real Christianity*. It took him nine years to write and his publisher thought that it wouldn't sell very well and so only printed 500 copies. It was published in April 1797 and by August went into five editions and sold 7,500 copies. It is a well-argued and passionate presentation of the truth of the Christian faith and the utter uselessness of man-made religion.

Unlike many of our politicians and educationalists today, as well as some of our church leaders, Wilberforce had a realistic, biblical view of human nature, a genuine understanding of the real problem and God's remedy. He saw that *all* men and women were in fact slaves. Their freedom was a delusion—they were slaves to sin and the devil (the 'hideous strength') which alone sufficiently explained the dreadful things in the world. As Jesus said in Matthew 15:18, 'what comes out of the mouth proceeds from the heart, and this defiles a person.' Wilberforce saw clearly that this could only be changed by divine intervention.

Wilberforce saw that all men and women were slaves; their freedom was a delusion

Wilberforce used both hands, the right hand of proclaiming the gospel, and the left hand of refuting present day ideas and values, using all the means at his disposal to effect change. This took great courage.

The same outlook is required today especially by those in positions of leadership and, more specifically, evangelical leadership. Thankfully there are some, like Bishop Michael Nazir-Ali in Britain, Os Guinness, David Wells and Carl Trueman in the States. But the silence from Anglican evangelical leaders on these issues is deafening. Whilst claiming to be the heirs of the nineteenth-century evangelicals, they do not seem to have their courage particularly when it comes to confronting the 'hideous strength' within the established church or in the wider culture. Speaking of the way a new Gnosticism has crept into the church's thinking about sexuality, Dr Gerald Bray's assessment is cutting but accurate when speaking of Anglican evangelicals:

> *Preaching the truth is necessary; but there must also be a speaking out*

> There is no common strategy, despite many meetings that are supposedly framing one, and we suspect that when the crunch comes, many in the leadership will do what they do best—run and hide (or as they would say, 'pray about it'). Spinelessness has long been the mark of the true Evangelical, and we must expect that it will be just as much in evidence this time around as it has been in the past.

Preaching *up* the truth is necessary but not sufficient; there must also be a speaking *out*. This is singularly lacking amongst the Anglican evangelical leadership and a continual source of disappointment and frustration to those who are seeking to contend in both church and culture.

In her article, 'Our Children As Gay Champions', Lisa Nolland points to another approach being adopted by evangelicals and its inevitable failure:

A popular approach of UK evangelical churches to this issue is to shun controversy while focusing on 'gospel love'. This approach is essentially free of ethical demands, and foregrounds PC [politically correct] positives while leaving the controversial bits, such as homosexuality, for later ... Problems with this approach include firstly the privileging of Christ's death and resurrection in such a way that his life and teaching, with their explicit and implicit ethical demands, are eclipsed. Our rendition of Jesus himself must now be censored! Secondly, this approach presupposes an adherence to a traditional Christian sex ethic which is rapidly vanishing among even the devout. Those who claim to affirm this ethic keep turning the volume down (or off!). Steve Chalke has many still-closeted allies in 'solid' churches. Many more are simply no longer sure or deduce that it must be a matter of little significance. Andrew Walker notes transitional stages from orthodoxy to 'progressivism': relativising the issue becomes being uncertain about it, refusing to speak publicly about and then being indifferent to it. Next comes acceptance, agreement then requirement. Thirdly, this approach fails to factor in the new 'normal' of many evangelical youngsters marinated now in all things gay. Those with dog collars and institutional buffers are somewhat protected. They seem too busy, stressed, pre-occupied with pastoral care and internal church issues and/or lack elemental curiosity to discover the depth of the rot, the extent of the loss. Something of a 'don't-ask-don't-tell' policy could be operant, even at a subconscious level.

Earlier attention was drawn to parallels between Christians living in pre-war Nazi Germany and our present situation, this also holds for the easy-going manner some evangelicals are adopting towards the Church of England as it blithely embraces the new norms of the secular culture. Here we have Gustav Heinemann writing in 1938:

> We have done nothing to awaken a genuine and credible readiness to give up the official church ... How much have we declared unbearable, and yet we bear it ... We are neither as an organisation nor as individuals prepared for anything other than that which we have had for generations ... In the best case, we are waiting for a great and utterly unignorable signal to break away. It will not come. There will only be signals in small doses, which will not bring us to a complete break.

Similarly, there will be no unignorable signal for those in the mixed denominations in which the 'hideous strength' continues to exercise its power.

Another parallel exists between the present and the 1930s in terms of leadership:

> Why was Churchill unwilling to ignore what was happening in Germany in the 1930s? What did he have which far more respectable opponents like Halifax lacked? The latter chose to turn a blind eye and thus tacitly collude and, after September 1939, actively appease. Churchill was

willing to know, which made all the difference. People may not be losing their lives but they are losing their jobs for being non-pc.

We have plenty of Halifaxes in the evangelical wing of the Church of England, where are the Churchills who will speak out as the Archbishop of Canterbury, Justin Welby, promotes LGBT concerns?

On 4 April 1967, Martin Luther King Jr, speaking of those church ministers, who for whatever reason, refused to speak out on the Vietnam War, said there 'Is a time when silence is betrayal.' One fears that there is a similar betrayal, however unintended, by some evangelical leaders today on some of the major issues facing the church and culture which we have been expounding in this book.

That silence must end.

Non nobis Domine

Kevin J. Vanhoozer in his essay, 'Sapiential Apologetics', speaks of the Christian apologist as the 'Knight of Faith.' He draws attention to the Apostle Paul as exemplifying what such a knight might look like, someone who commends the faith in word and deed. A knight was skilled in wielding his weapons, both offensively and defensively as well as displaying certain virtues. One of the greatest virtues, in addition to courage is humility. The motto of the Knights Templar was *Non nobis Domine non nobis sed Nomini Tuo da gloriam*—'Not unto us O Lord not unto us but to your Name give glory' (Psalm

115:1). It is in that spirit that the Christians must conduct themselves against the ideology and forces of spiritual darkness which confront us today. To attempt to do it in our own strength would be to engage in the same folly as the builders of the Tower of Babel. This is *God's* battle and we are to employ God's methods of prayer, proclamation, persuasion and be willing to undergo pain in doing so. The result will be that whatever the particular outcome for Christians (such as martyrdom and estrangement), God's glory will be assured.

James Davison Hunter has argued that what ultimately makes the decisive difference in changing the world are not simply great men with great ideas, but ideas embedded in culture-producing institutions. It can hardly be said that the church in Britain, including the Church of England, qualifies. Hunter contends that the church should be less concerned with seizing power by political means and instead should seek to be 'faithfully present.' He writes, 'The vocation of the church is to bear witness to and to be a faithful embodiment of the coming kingdom of God.' In other words, it is to proclaim and defend the central truths in Christ as we outlined earlier and to live them out. It will not do to surrender to the non-realities of cultural Marxism or any other ideology which sets itself over and against God's kingdom (including those theologies which use kingdom language to promote its anti-kingdom agenda, i.e. those of the anti-Christ).

Since in our present cultural climate Christians will feel

the pressure to keep their heads down and mouths shut, as hoped for by the cultural Marxists, gospel integrity is crucial. This is a quality of life formed by the Holy Spirit enabling each church congregation to become a lived 'plausibility structure.' We certainly need to argue and assert our theology but we also have to live it. It is not just the integrity of our message which counts but the integrity of the messengers. Postmoderns may not be too fussed about our arguments but they may find it more difficult to argue with our lives if they bear the mark of gospel authenticity. It is these gatherings (churches), gathered by God through the gospel in power by the Spirit that embody the gospel and which, in the words of John Chrysostom, 'puts to flight' the world.

> *Gospel integrity is crucial in our present cultural climate*

On being against the world for the world

For such communities to be formed, communities that will stand over and against the world, for the world, three things are essential.

First, *a praying people*.

Referring to the Magisterial Reformation in *Renaissance*, Os Guinness writes,

> The Reformation ... did not come then, and in our much needed reformation today will not come, when Christian

leaders sit around a board table with yellow pads and outline their vision from 'mission' to 'measurable outcomes.' Rather, it will come when men and women of God wrestle with God as Jacob wrestled with the angel—wrestling with God with their consciences, with their times and with the state of the church in their times, until out of that intense wrestling comes an experience of God that is shattering and all-decisive, and the source of what may later once again be termed a reformation.

The apostle Paul concludes his great passage on spiritual warfare in Ephesians 6:10–20 with the call to prayer of all kinds on all occasions. One may be excused for thinking that for some evangelicals, prayer is an afterthought, an add on to when we have done all the business through their conferences, collaborations and compromises. This will not do. *Non nobis* leads to prayer.

Second, a *literate leadership*.

To speak of a literate leadership is not to be taken literally! I am assuming most church leaders in the West can read and write. By literacy I am referring to the ability to read things *rightly* which involves more than being able to pronounce words on a page or understand the meaning of a poster. It involves possessing basic information (knowledge), and knowing how to apply that information (wisdom) so we might thrive.

To be sure, there is the need for biblical literacy. This is the ability to interpret particular passages in the light of the whole (*canonical literacy*), following a story or theme which recognises unity and diversity, yet recognising that the Old Testament and New Testament belong together (*biblical theology*), understanding the main truths of Scripture and how they relate (*systematic theology*) as well as reading our world in the light of the biblical text knowing that for whatever superficial differences in culture, Christians today still stand in the same flow of redemption-history (*pastoral theology*).

However, there is also the need for *cultural literacy*. Culture is, as Vanhoozer explains in *The Pastor as Public Theologian*, 'the world of meaning in which a people dwell, a world presented in various works of meaning ... that communicate a society's beliefs and values.' If pastors do not know the culture in which people 'live, move and have their being' they will not be able to minister to them effectively. And if this doesn't

> *If pastors do not know the culture there will be a disconnect between what is preached on Sunday and encountered on Monday*

happen then there will be a disconnect between what is preached on Sunday and what is encountered on Monday. One of the maxims of war is 'know your enemy,' and presumably if one is to engage effectively, one must also 'know the territory' in which the fight is to take place. Not educating Christians about what is taking place in their society, (exposing the influence of the 'hideous strength') will be like sending a soldier out with the 'sword of the Spirit' (we have 'preached the Word' after all), without instructing them how to wield it and against whom. Vanhoozer explains:

> The so-called 'culture wars' are really a symptom of a deeper problem: the fact that Christians struggle not against flesh and blood, nor against food and film, but against the powers and principalities that seek to capture our minds and hearts. Cultural literacy is the ability to 'read' or make sense of what is happening in our contemporary situation.

Evangelical church leaders must get up to speed on what is happening to help those to whom it is happening.

Thirdly, *a changed community*.

Vanhoozer again:

> At the end of the day … the Knight of faith is not a crusader, a wielding force, but a knight of the Lord's Table, one who knows how to live out union and communion in Christ. Knights of the Lord's Table are grateful realists who joyfully affirm their faith in Christ, and are ready to put their faith to all sorts of critical tests, intellectual, existential and social.

The people of Babel then and now live a lie, adopting beliefs and practices which were at odds with the reality as God created it. The people of the Bride are meant to be people who have 'got real,' who know the reality in Christ and live according to it as they gather and as they go out into the world which Christ came to redeem. This also entails supporting those brothers and sisters who are seeking to refute the lie and promote the truth.

On a practical level, could not churches at least encourage their members to support those people and bodies seeking to do this, like the Christian Institute and Christian Concern? Perhaps some churches could go further and ensure part of their annual outside giving is directed towards them. This does not mean we will agree with every detail of what they say or do, any more than they would with what we say or do, but they are on the side of the angels and deserve not only our respect but active support.

When all is said and done

When all is said and done there will always be *more* to be said and *more* to be done. What we are facing today is a 'hideous strength' far more fearsome and all-embracing than Lewis envisaged over 70 years ago. The technology available is far more potent and far-reaching in its ability to capture imaginations and minds than at any point in the world's history. The political will of the opponents of Christianity is strong and unrelenting. The church by and large appears confused and compromised. The stakes are incredibly high: nothing less than the survival of a civilization and the eternal well-being of countless souls.

What are we to do?

We have already outlined some things which are necessary and these cannot be shirked. But what we must exercise is precisely the very thing that was denied at Babel, faith in God. As Os Guiness explains in *Renaissance*, 'The time has come to trust God, move out, sharing and demonstrating the good news, following his call and living out our callings in every area of our lives, and then leave the outcome to him.'

Returning to Lewis's story with which we began and the episode of Genesis 11 which the story illustrates—it was not by devising some clever scheme to out manoeuvre the plotters of N.I.C.E that final victory was accomplished, nor was it by God searching out a few righteous men like Noah that the builders of the Tower were thrown into confusion; it was ultimately by a special intervention of God. We can say that God has already intervened in the person of his Son, and that he continues, as he sees fit, to intervene by the work of his Spirit as the gospel is proclaimed and lived out in all its fullness. We pray that he will do so again so that it will not be to us, but to him that the glory goes.

Works Cited

Adler, Jerry, et al., 'Taking Offense', *Newsweek*, 24 December 1990

Admin, 'Catholic Priest Timothy Radcliffe's Submission to the C of E Inquiry into Human Sexuality', *Centre for the Study of Christianity and Sexuality*, 18 February 2014 <http://christianityandsexuality.org/?tag=pilling-report>

Adorno, T. W., *The Authoritarian Personality* (W. W. Norton & Co, 1994)

Arendt, Hannah, *Eichmann in Jerusalem: A Report on the Banality of Evil* (Penguin, 1977)

Ashenden, Gavin, 'Sinister agenda to replace families with Big Brother' <https://ashenden.org/2018/03/15/when-the-silly-becomes-the-sinister-the-latest-round-in-the-culture-wars>

Austin, James, *The Tower of Babel in Genesis: How the Tower of Babel Narrative Influences the Theology of Genesis and the Bible* (West Bow Press, 2012)

Barnett, Victoria, *For the Soul of the People* (Oxford University Press, 1992)

Bartholomew, Craig G., *The Drama of Scripture: Finding Our Place in the Biblical Story* (SPCK, 2014)

Billings, Rachel M., 'How to Survive the Apocalypse', *Reformation 21*, August 2016 <http://www.reformation21.org/articles/how-to-survive-the-apocalypse.php>

Blamires, Harry, *Where do we Stand? An Examination of the Christian's Position in the Modern World* (SPCK, 1980)

Bray, Gerald, 'Editorial: Mind over Matter?', *Churchman*, 130.2 (2016)

Breshears, Jefrey D., *The Origin of Cultural Marxism and Political Correctness,* Part 1 (The Areopagus, 2016)

———., *The Origin of Cultural Marxism and Political Correctness,* Part 2 (The Areopagus, 2016)

Brunner, Emile, *Christianity and Civilization* (James Clarke, 2009)

Cameron, Nigel M. de S., and Pamela F. Sims, *Abortion: the Crisis in Morals and Medicine* (IVP, 1986)

Carson, D. A., 'A Sketch of the Factors Determining Current Hermeneutical Debate in Cross-Cultural Contexts', *Biblical Interpretation and the Church: The Problem of Contextualization* (Wipf and Stock, 2002)

Chesterton, G. K., *The Everlasting Man* (Martino Fine Books, 2010)

Colson, Charles, *Lies That Go Unchallenged in Popular Culture* (Tyndale, 2005)

Davison Hunter, James, *To Change the World: The Irony, Tragedy and Possibility of Christianity in the Late Modern World* (Oxford University Press, 2010)

Davidson, Mike, '"Gay Conversion therapy"—Is It Harmful? Frequently Asked Questions', 22 June 2017 <*Core Issues Trust* https://www.core-issues.org/news/ what-is-conversion-therapy>

Dawkins, Richard, 'The Ultra Violet Garden', *Royal Institute Christmas Lecture No 4*, 1991

Douglas, Mary, *Leviticus as Literature* (Oxford University Press, 2001)

———., *Purity and Danger: An Analysis of the Concepts of Pollution and Taboo* (Routledge, 1984)

Dreher, Rod, 'Sex After Christianity: Gay marriage is not just a social revolution but a cosmological one', *The American Conservative*, 11 April 2013 <http://www.theamericanconservative.com/articles/ sex-after-christianity>

D'Souza, Dinesh, *What's so great about Christianity* (Regnery Publishing, 2007)

Eaton, George, 'Why Antonio Gramsci is the Marxist thinker for our times', *New Statesman*, 5 February 2018 <https://www. newstatesman.com/culture/ observations/ 2018/02/why-antonio-gramsci-marxist-thinker-our-times>

Ehrenstein, David, 'More than Friends', *Los Angeles Magazine*, May 1996

Francis, Thomas, 'Animal Instincts', *Miami New Times*, 20 August 2009 <http://www.miaminewtimes.com/news/animal-instincts-6378144#Comments>

Fuller, Andrew, *The Works of Andrew Fuller* (Banner of Truth, 2007)

Guinness, Os, 'Christian Courage and the Struggle for Civilization', *C.S. Lewis Institute Broadcast Talks*, 2.4 (2017), 1–15

——., *Dining with the Devil: The Mega Church Movement Flirts with Modernity* (Baker, 1993)

——., *Prophetic Untimeliness: A Challenge to the Idol of Relevance* (Baker Books, 2003)

——., *Renaissance: The Power of the Gospel However Dark the Times* (IVP, 2014)

——., *The Gravedigger File* (Hodder & Stoughton, 1983)

——., *Time for Truth: Living in a world of Lies, Hype and Spin* (IVP, 2000)

Haldane, J.B.S., 'Eugenics and Social Reform', *Possible Worlds* (Transaction Publishers, 2001)

Hale, Virginia, 'Parent Backlash As Cross-Dressing Men Sent Into Primary Schools To "Promote Tolerance"', *Breitbart*, 25 February 2018 <http://www.breitbart.com/london/2018/02/25/backlash-drag-queens-primary-school>

Hook, Sidney, 'Marxism', *Dictionary of the History of Ideas* (Charles Scribner, 1973)

Hooper, Walter, *C.S. Lewis: A Companion & Guide* (Harper, 1996)

Hooykaas, R. J., *Religion and the Rise of Modern Science* (Eerdmans, 1974)

James, Scott, 'Many Successful Gay Marriages Share an Open Secret', *The New York Times*, 29 January 2010 <https://www.nytimes.com/2010/01/29/us/29sfmetro.html>

Jones, Peter, 'A Response to Rod Dreher's "Sex After Christianity"', April 2014, <http://www.reformation21.org/featured/a-response-to-rod-drehers-sex-after-christianity.php>

Jones, Will, *The Conservative Woman*, 'The C of E's Same-Sex Marriage of Convenience', 3 December 2017, <https://www.conservativewoman.co.uk/will-jones-c-es-sex-marriage-convenience/?utm_source=TCW+Daily+Email&utm_campaign=b4bb06aa59-RSS_DAILY_EMAIL&utm_medium=email&utm_term=0_a63ccaicc5-b4bb06aa59–556076645>

Joustra, Robert, and Alissa Wilkinson, *How to Survive the Apocalypse: Zombies, Cylons, Faith, and Politics at the End of the World* (Eerdmans, 2016)

Kelley, D. M., *Why Conservative Churches are Growing: A Study in Sociology of Religion* (Harper & Row, 1972)

Kirk, Marshall, and Hunter Madsen, *After the Ball: How America Will Conquer It's Fear and Hatred of Gays in the 90's* (Plume Books, 1989)

Kuby, Gabriele, *The Global Sexual Revolution: The Destruction of Freedom in the Name of Freedom* (LifeSite, 2015)

Lewis, C.S., 'Bulverism', *First and Second Things* (Fount, 1985)

——., 'Christian Apologetics', *God in the Dock: Essays on Theology and Ethics* (Eerdmans, 2014)

——., *Of Other Worlds: Essays and Stories*, (Harvest Books, 2002)

——., *That Hideous Strength* (Harper Collins, 2005)

——., *The Abolition of Man* (Fount, 1978)

Lind, William S., 'Further Readings in the Frankfurt School', *Political Correctness: A Short History of an Ideology* <http://www. nationalists.org/pdf/political_ correctness_a_short_history_of_ an_ideology.pdf>

Lowman, Pete, 'Chronicles of Heaven Unshackled', <https://www. bethinking.org/your-studies/chronicles-of-heaven-unshackled/5-that-hideous-strength>

Mackay, D. M., 'Man as a mechanism', *The Open Mind: A Scientist in God's World* (IVP, 1988)

Mann, Julian, *Christians in the Community of the Dome* (Evangelical Press, 2017)

Marcuse, Herbert, *Eros and Civilization: A Philosophical Inquiry into Freud* (Beacon Press, 1974)

——., 'Repressive Tolerance', *A Critique of Pure Tolerance* (Beacon Press, 1965)

McGrath, Alister, *C.S. Lewis: A Life: Eccentric Genius, Reluctant Prophet* (Hodder & Stoughton, 2013)

Minnicino, Michael J., 'The New Dark Age: The Frankfurt School and "Political Correctness"', *Fidelio*, 1.1 (1992)

Mohler, Al, 'After the Ball—Why the Homosexual Movement Has Won', 3 June 2004 <http://www.freerepublic.com/focus/religion/1147428/posts>

Montgomery, Kathryn C., *Target: Prime Time: Advocacy Groups and the Struggle over Entertainment Television* (Oxford University Press, 1989)

Naugle, David K., 'The Devils in Our World', 16 July 2016 <http://www.cslewis.com/the-devils-in-our-world>

Niebuhr, Reinhold, *Does Civilization Need Religion? A Study in the Social Resources and Limitations of Religion in Modern Life* (Wipf & Stock, 2010)

Nolland, Lisa, 'Children as Gay Champions?', *Evangelicals Now*, September 2015

——., 'While the Church Sleeps ...', *Evangelicals Now*, September 2016

O'Donovan, Oliver, *Transsexualism and Christian Marriage* (Grove Booklet on Ethics, 1982)

Oliphint, K. Scott 'The Most Moved Mediator', *Themelios,* 30.1 (2004)

Ortlund, Gavin, 'Conversion in C.S. Lewis's That Hideous Strength,' *Themelios* 41.1 (2016)

Orwell, George, 'The Scientists Take Over: Review of *That Hideous Strength*', *Manchester Evening News*, 16 August 1945 <http://www.lewisiana.nl/orwell>

Sandlin, P. Andrew, 'How Modern Marxism is Libertarian', 29 August 2017 <https://docsandlin.com/2017/08/29/how-modern-marxism-is-libertarian>

Paglia, Camille , *Sex, Art and American Culture* (Vintage Books, 1992)

Piper, John, *Spectacular Sins* (Crossway, 2008)

Rieff, Philip, *The Triumph of the Therapeutic: Uses of Faith After Freud* (ISI Books, 2006)

Roberts, Matthew, 'Why Pelagianism Matters (including for the Church of England)', 18 July 2017 <https://matthewpwroberts. wordpress.com/2017/07/18/why-pelagianism-matters-including-to-the-church-of-england>

Robertson, David, 'The Lion has Whimpered', <https://theweeflea. com/2018/03/ 28/the-lion-has-whimpered/amp/?__twitter_ impression=true>

Russell, Bertrand *Marriage and Morals* (Routledge, 2009)

Sammons, Martha C., *A Far Off Country: A Guide to C.S. Lewis' Fantasy Fiction* (University Press of America, 2000)

Stark, Rodney, and Roger Finke, *Acts of Faith: Explaining the Human Side of Religion* (University of California Press, 2000)

Stenmark, Michael, *Scientism: Science, Ethics and Religion* (Ashgate, 2001)

Tan, Chik Kaw, 'Fundamental shifts in the General Synod', 20 July 2017 <https://www.gafcon.org/news/fundamental-shifts-in-the-general-synod>

Taylor, Charles, *Modern Social Imaginaries* (Duke University Press, 2004)

Tinker, Melvin, *Touchy Topics* (Evangelical Press, 2016)

Trueman, Carl, 'The Banality of Evil', *Minority Report* (Christian Focus Publications, 2008)

———., 'The Joy of Paglian Sex', *Postcards From Palookaville*, 18

September 2017 <http://www.alliancenet.org/mos/postcards-from-palookaville/the-joy-of-paglian-sex#.WxaooS_MwWo>

Vanhoozer, Kevin J., *From Physics to Metaphysics: Imagining the World that Scripture Imagines—An after dinner talk to the Henry Fellows and Stott Award Winners,* 18 January 2018 <http://henrycenter. tiu.edu/resource/from-physics-to-metaphysics-imagining-the-world-that-scripture-imagines>

——., *Pictures at a Theological Exhibition* (IVP, 2016)

——., 'Sapiential Apologetics', *Pictures at a Theological Exhibition* (IVP, 2016)

——., *The Pastor as Public Theologian: Reclaiming a Lost Vision* (Baker, 2015)

Walton, John H., 'Ancient Near Eastern Background Studies', *Dictionary for Theological Interpretation of the Bible* (Baker, 2005)

Ward, Keith, *The Turn of the Tide: Christianity in Britain Today* (BBC Books, 1986)

Welby, Justin, *Reimagining Britain: Foundations for Hope* (Bloomsbury Continuum, 2018)

Wells, David F., *The Courage to be Protestant: Truth-Lovers, Marketers, and Emergents in the Postmodern World* (Eerdmans, 2008)

Wilberforce, William, *Real Christianity* (Bethany House, 2006)

Williams, Rowan, '"That Hideous Strength": A Reassessment', *C.S. Lewis and His Circle: Essays and Memoirs from the Oxford C.S. Lewis Society* (Oxford University Press, 2015)